Microsoft®

Access® 2010 Plain & Simple

Curtis D. Frye

Published with the authorization of Microsoft Corporation by:
O'Reilly Media, Inc.
1005 Gravenstein Highway North
Sebastopol, California 95472

Printed and bound in the United States of America.

2 3 4 5 6 7 8 9 10 QG 7 6 5 4 3 2

Microsoft Press titles may be purchased for educational, business or sales promotional use. Online editions are also available for most titles (*http://my.safaribooksonline.com*). For more information, contact our corporate/institutional sales department: (800) 998-9938 or *corporate@oreilly.com*. Visit our website at *microsoftpress.oreilly.com*. Send comments to *mspinput@microsoft.com*.

Acquisitions and Developmental Editor: Kenyon Brown
Production Editor: Loranah Dimant
Copy Editor: Nancy Sixsmith
Editorial Production: Octal Publishing, Inc.
Technical Reviewer: Mark Reddin
Compositor: Ron Bilodeau
Illustrator: Robert Romano
Indexer: Ginny Munroe

978-0-7356-2730-7

[2012-04-06]

Contents

4

Creating a Database   25

5

Customizing Fields   47

9 Creating Reports 127

10 Beautifying Forms and Reports 145

11   Creating Charts in Access 2010   173

12   Interacting with Other Programs   185

What do you think of this book? We want to hear from you!

Microsoft is interested in hearing your feedback so we can continually improve our books and learning resources for you. To participate in a brief online survey, please visit:

www.microsoft.com/learning/booksurvey/

1

Introduction: About This Book

If you want to get the most from your computer and your software with the least amount of time and effort—and who doesn't?—this book is for you. You'll find *Microsoft® Access® 2010 Plain & Simple* to be a straightforward, easy-to-read reference tool. With the premise that your computer should work for you, not you for it, this book's purpose is to help you get your work done quickly and efficiently so that you can get away from the computer and live your life.

No Computerese!

Let's face it: When there's a task you don't know how to do but you need to get it done in a hurry, or when you're stuck in the middle of a task and can't figure out what to do next, there's nothing more frustrating than having to read page after page of technical background material. You want the information you need—nothing more, nothing less—and you want it now! It should be easy to find and understand.

That's what this book is all about. It's written in plain English—no jargon. There's no single task in the book that takes more than a couple of pages. Just look up the task in the index or the table of contents, turn to the page, and you'll find the information you need laid out in an illustrated step-by-step format. You won't get bogged down by the whys and wherefores: Just follow the steps and get your work done.

Occasionally, you might have to turn to another page if the procedure you're working on is accompanied by a "See Also." That's because a lot of tasks overlap, and I didn't want to keep repeating myself. Some useful "Tips" are scattered here and there, and a "Try This" or a "Caution" is thrown in once in a while, but by and large I've tried to remain true to the heart and soul of a Plain & Simple book, which is that the information you need is available to you at a glance.

Useful Tasks...

Whether you use Microsoft Access 2010 at home or on the road, I've tried to pack this book with procedures for everything I could think of that you might want to do, from the simplest tasks to some of the more esoteric ones.

...And the Easiest Way to Do Them

Another thing I've tried to do in this book is to identify and document the easiest way to accomplish a task. Access 2010 often provides a multitude of methods to accomplish a single end result—which can be daunting or delightful, depending on the way you like to work. If you tend to stick with one favorite and familiar approach, I think the methods described in this book are the way to go. If you like trying out alternative techniques, go ahead! The intuitiveness of Access 2010 invites exploration, and you're likely to discover ways of doing things that you think are easier or that you like better than mine. If you do, that's great! It's exactly what the developers of Access 2010 had in mind when they provided so many alternatives.

A Quick Overview

Your computer probably came with Access 2010 preinstalled, but if you have to install it yourself, the setup routine makes installation so simple that you won't need my help anyway. So, unlike many computer books, this one doesn't start with installation instructions and a list of system requirements.

Next, you don't need to read this book in any particular order. You can jump in, get the information you need, and then close the book and keep it near your computer until the next time you need to know how to get something done. But that doesn't mean the information is scattered about with wild abandon. The book is organized so that the tasks you want to accomplish are arranged in two levels. You'll find the general type of task you're looking for under a main section title such as "Creating a New Database," "Getting Help," "Exporting Data to a Text File," and so on. Then, in each of those sections, the smaller tasks within the main task are arranged in a loose progression from the simplest to the more complex.

Section 1, which you're reading now, introduces *Microsoft Access 2010 Plain & Simple* and tells you what to expect in this book. Section 2 covers what's new in Access 2010, from the new Backstage View that helps you manage your databases effectively to the new ways you can summarize your data visually. Sections 3 and 4 cover the basics of operating a database: starting Access 2010 and shutting it down, sizing and arranging program windows, getting help from within the program and on the Web, what types of objects are available in an Access 2010 database, and the role each of those objects fulfills. There's also a lot of useful information about designing and creating a new database, either from scratch or by using built-in database templates; navigating within a database; creating relationships between tables; and getting data from other Access 2010 databases.

Section 5 is all about customizing your table fields. You'll discover the different types offi fields available to you; how to add, delete, and rearrange fields; and how to make data entry easier for you and your colleagues. You'll find the information helpful whether you want to change how a field displays its data, set a default value for a field, ensure that the data entered into the field is appropriate for that field, or enter table data by picking the proper value from a list.

Section 6 focuses on working with entire tables, rather than individual fields in a table. Here's where you'll find information about entering data quickly, finding and replacing table text, and modifying how Access 2010 displays your data in a table. There's also a short section here on filtering a table's contents, which lets you limit the data displayed to exactly what you need to make a decision.

Sections 7 through 10 are all about building database objects to take best advantage of your data: creating forms, which let you present your data in an attractive format and enter new table records; building reports, which summarize your data and make it easy to create mailing labels; defining queries, which let you ask specific questions of your table data; and changing the appearance of your forms and reports to make them more attractive or to conform with a company's color scheme. Section 10 describes how you can use conditional formatting, which is new in Access 2010, to add visual cues that enable you and your colleagues to evaluate report data at a glance.

Section 11 shows you how to summarize your Access 2010 data visually by creating charts. Charts enable you to summarize large data collections quickly, compare historical data to current trends, and provide context for when you discuss specific data points from your tables.

Section 12 is about interacting with other programs, such as by including files created in other programs in your databases, adding pictures to forms and reports, or including Microsoft Excel charts in your database. You will also find out how to exchange data with other programs, whether that means exporting Access 2010 table or query data to another program or reading data from another program's files into Access 2010.

The final sections, 13 through 15, deal with more advanced topics: administering your database so you can, if necessary, identify the data that is open for anyone to look over and separate that data from tables or queries that might contain more sensitive information; creating navigation forms that make it easier to move around in your databases; customizing Access 2010 by changing the items that appear on the program's Quick Access Toolbar and the Ribbon user interface; and creating forms that let you dynamically reorganize your data. If you think these tasks sound complex, rest assured they're not—Access 2010 makes them so easy that you'll sail right through.

A Few Assumptions

I had to make a few educated guesses about the audience when I started writing this book. Perhaps you use Access just for personal reasons—keeping track of your books, music, contacts, and so on. Perhaps you use Access at work to maintain records of your inventory, customers, and the orders they place. Or maybe you run a small home-based business. Taking all these possibilities into account, I assumed that you'd need to know how to create, modify, and work with all the basic Access database objects; to administer the database; and to share the data on the Internet or over your company's internal network.

Another assumption I made is that you have an inherent curiosity about what you can do with Access 2010. Rather than show you how to perform specific tasks, such as designing a database to track client interactions or customer orders, I assumed you wanted a broad base of experience from which to work. I hope that the tasks in this book provide a solid foundation for you to learn more about Access and what it can do for you.

A Final Word (or Two)

I had three goals in writing this book:

- **Whatever you want to do, I want the book to help you get it done.**

- **I want the book to help you discover how to do things you didn't know you wanted to do.**

- **And, finally, if I've achieved the first two goals, I'll be well on the way to the third, which is for my book to help you enjoy using Access 2010. I think that's the best gift I could give you to thank you for buying my book.**

I hope you'll have as much fun reading and using *Microsoft Access 2010 Plain & Simple* as I've had writing it. The best way to learn is by doing, and that's how I hope you'll use this book.

Jump right in!

2

What's New in Access 2010?

One of the first things you'll notice about Microsoft Access 2010 is that the program incorporates the Microsoft Fluent interface, also known as the Ribbon, which was introduced in Access 2007. If you used Access 2003 or an earlier version of Access, you'll need to spend only a little bit of time working with the new user interface to bring yourself back up to your usual proficiency. If you used Access 2007, you'll immediately notice one significant change: the Microsoft Office Button, located at the top left corner of the program window in Access 2007, has been replaced by the File tab.

This section of the book introduces many of the new features in Access 2010: the new Backstage view you use to manage your files; new templates and Application Parts you can use to build databases more quickly; new abilities to customize the Ribbon user interface; new Office Themes, which make formatting simpler and more consistent; and new data visualization techniques, which include Office Themes and conditional formatting.

All these improvements combine to make Access 2010 a friendly yet powerful program you can use effectively right out of the box, with a little help from *Microsoft Access 2010 Plain & Simple*.

Managing Access Settings and Files in Backstage View

After releasing the 2007 Microsoft Office System, the Microsoft Office User Experience team re-examined the programs' user interfaces to determine how they could be improved. During this process, they discovered that it was possible to divide user tasks into two categories: "in" tasks, such as table and report creation, which affect the contents of the database directly; and "out" tasks, such as saving and printing, which could be considered file management tasks.

When the User Experience and Access teams focused their attention on the Access 2007 user interface, they discovered that several file management tasks were sprinkled among the Ribbon tabs that contained content-related tasks. The Access team moved all the file management tasks under the File tab, which users can click to display these commands in the new Backstage view.

Customizing the Access 2010 User Interface

When the Microsoft Office User Experience team designed the Ribbon interface for Access 2007, they allowed you to modify the program window by adding and removing commands on the Quick Access Toolbar. In Access 2010, you can still modify the Quick Access Toolbar, but you also have much more ability to change the Ribbon interface. Users can hide or display built-in Ribbon tabs, change the order of built-in Ribbon tabs, add custom control groups to a Ribbon tab, and create custom Ribbon tabs that, in turn, can contain custom groups. These custom groups provide easy access to existing Ribbon controls as well as custom controls that run macros stored in the database.

Creating Databases Using Improved Templates

Every user is different, but the Access product team has discovered through its research that users frequently create the same types of databases. Some users create databases to track upcoming events; others use them to track the students and faculty at an educational institution; and still others track marketing projects, sales, and tasks they've been assigned.

Access 2010 comes with a number of built-in database templates you can use to create a database that is prepopulated with objects suited for your application. Access 2010 includes two types of database templates: regular databases and Web databases. A regular database is stored on your computer and can just be used just by someone who has permission to use your computer and to view your files. A Web database can be used on your computer, or it can be stored on a Microsoft SharePoint server. Uploading a database to a SharePoint server enables other users to interact with the database using a Web browser. Uploading a database to a SharePoint site is beyond the scope of this book, but you can use databases you create from Web database templates on your computer as if they were regular databases.

Building Databases by Re-Using Application Parts

After you've used Access 2010 for a while, you'll almost certainly find that you can use database objects you created previously as the basis for new database objects. Access 2010 comes with a number of built-in form templates, called Application Parts, which you can use to accelerate your work. When you click the Create tab on the Ribbon and then click Application Parts, Access 2010 displays the Application Parts that are available to you. Some of the Application Parts are blank forms you can link to another table, but the Contacts, Issues, and Tasks templates in the Quick Start section of the gallery enable you to create and link forms by moving through the steps of a form creation wizard.

Creating Navigation Forms

Most databases contain multiple tables, forms, reports, and queries. If you created the database, it can be difficult to remember which elements perform which functions within your database. Your life gets even more complicated if you're using a database someone else created, or even one you created some time ago. In those instances, you'll need to examine the database's contents to discover (or rediscover) how to enter and analyze your data.

In Access 2007 and earlier versions of the program, you could create switchboard forms to guide users to the objects they should use for certain tasks. The procedure for creating switchboards was cumbersome, so the Access program team created navigation forms. You can drag forms and reports onto a navigation form, which means you and your colleagues can gain easy access to the elements that enable you to enter, edit, and summarize your database's contents.

Formatting Database Objects Using Office Themes

Access 2010 includes new capabilities to apply attractive color schemes to your database objects. You could always change the appearance of your forms and reports, but Access 2010 includes collections of complementary colors called Office Themes. You can use the Office Themes that are installed with Access 2010 to format your database objects, or you can create your own themes that reflect your personal design choices or your company's official color scheme.

Gaining Insights into Data Using Conditional Formatting

Microsoft Access has always provided powerful tools you can use to manage and summarize substantial data collections. Access 2010 extends those capabilities by allowing you to apply conditional formats that summarize your data visually. A conditional format changes to reflect the numeric values in a report field. For example, if you create a report to summarize your company's sales performance, you could define conditional formats that indicate whether your company's performance exceeded its goals, met expectations, or fell short.

Defining Calculated Fields Using the Improved Expression Builder

In Access 2007 and earlier versions, you could define a field's value as a function of the values in other fields. For example, you could calculate sales tax due on a purchase by multiplying the order's total price by the appropriate sales tax rate. To create this type of field, called a calculated field, you use the Expression Builder to define the calculation. Unfortunately, the Expression Builder in Access 2007 was somewhat difficult to use because of its crowded user interface and lack of contextual help tools.

In Access 2010, the improved Expression Builder provides a much cleaner user experience. Rather than force you to guess which commands you can use when you create an expression, the Expression Builder makes available only those commands that can be used in the current expression. The Expression Builder also offers to complete the commands you enter using IntelliSense, which enables you to enter your expressions more quickly and with fewer typing errors.

3

Introducing
Access 2010

Microsoft Access 2010 is designed to help you store, combine, and ask questions of large collections of data relevant to your business or your home life. You can create databases to track products and sales for a garden supply company, or, just as easily, build databases to keep track of your books and holiday card lists. Regardless of the specific use you have in mind, Access 2010 is a versatile program you can use to store and retrieve data quickly.

Working with Access 2010 is pretty straightforward. The program has a number of templates you can use to create entire databases or just parts of them. You also have the freedom to create databases and their components from scratch, giving you the flexibility you need to build any database.

This section of the book covers the basics: what a database is and how it works, starting Access 2010, shutting it down, opening databases, displaying database objects, and getting help using Access 2010. There's also an overall view of the Access 2010 window with labels for the most important parts of the program. You can use that image as a touchstone for learning more about Access 2010.

Introducing Databases

Storing Data on Index Cards

Before computers, a popular way to store data was on index cards. If you ran a gardening supply store, you could keep track of your products by creating a card for each product, dividing the cards into product categories, and then alphabetizing the cards in each section by product name. Each card would contain relevant data such as the product's name, unique identifier, category, price, description, and the supplier's name and phone number.

To find all the products from a specific supplier, you either needed to keep track of the products on a separate sheet of paper or go through the cards and pull every one representing a product made by that supplier.

Storing Data on the Computer

If you store the same data on the computer, however, you can find all the products from a specific supplier much more easily. As an example, you might create a Microsoft Word table with a column for each type of data you want to store.

With the list in a Word table, you can change the order of the table rows to group all the products from one supplier together; all you need to do then is scroll down through the table until you find the products from the supplier you want.

Using Word to store your data isn't the best solution, however. One limitation is that there's no way to combine information from two tables, so you need to write the supplier's phone number in every row representing a product from that supplier. If that phone number changes, you need to change the phone number entry in every table row representing a product from that supplier.

Storing Data in a Database

Databases, by contrast, are designed to combine data from several sources into a single table. Once data is entered into a table, it can be combined with other tables in the database to produce valuable information. It's possible, for example, to store information about suppliers in one table and information about purchase orders in another table. If a supplier changes its phone number, you need to change the phone number only once.

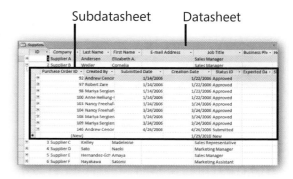

Subdatasheet   Datasheet

Starting Access 2010

After you install Access 2010 on your computer, you can run it to create new databases or to work with existing databases. There are two easy ways to run Access 2010: You can start it from the Start menu or by double-clicking a shortcut on your desktop. Regardless of the method you choose, you end up with the power of an Access 2010 database at your fingertips in the few seconds it takes your computer to start the program.

Start Access 2010

1. Click the Start button on the taskbar.

2. Click All Programs.

3. Click Microsoft Office.

4. Click Microsoft Access 2010.

Create a Shortcut for Access 2010

① Click the Start button on the taskbar.

② Click All Programs.

③ Click Microsoft Office.

④ Right-click Microsoft Access 2010.

⑤ Point to Send To.

⑥ Click Desktop (create shortcut).

⑦ Press the Escape key twice to close the menu.

Tip ✓

You can rename a shortcut by right-clicking it, clicking Rename on the shortcut menu that appears, typing a new name for the shortcut, and pressing Enter.

Surveying the Access 2010 Window

- The title bar displays the name of the database and the window control buttons.

- The tabs on the Ribbon enable you to display different types of commands based on the category you select.

- The Ribbon contains commands that reflect the active Contextual tab, your position in the database, and the selected objects.

- The Navigation Pane displays database objects of the type you select.

- The object window displays any open database objects.

- The status bar indicates the progress of any ongoing processes.

Main tab   Ribbon   Title bar   Minimize   Restore   Close

Navigation Pane   Status bar   Object window

Opening a Database

When you start Access 2010, the program opens in Backstage view. A list of recently opened files appears on the left edge of the window, below the File tab. You can select the file you want to open from the list that appears. If the file you want isn't on that list, click Open to display the Open dialog box. From the Open dialog box, you can navigate to the folder with the database you want to open.

Open a Database on Startup

1. Start Microsoft Access 2010.

2. Click Open.

3. Navigate to the folder with the database you want to open.

4. Double-click the file you want to open.

Open a Recently Used Database

(1) Start Microsoft Access 2010.

(2) Click Recent.

(3) Click the database you want to open.

Tip

The names of the last four databases you opened appear in the
File tab menu, just above the Info item.

Viewing Multiple Database Objects

Access 2010 enables you to work with multiple database objects efficiently. In Access 2010, the program displays a tab representing each open object at the top of the object window. If you want to display an object that is currently hidden, you can click that object's tab to display it. When you display an object in the object window, you can close the object by clicking its Close button (located at the top-right corner of the object window).

Close a Database Object

1. Click the Close button to close the displayed database object.

Scroll Within a Database Object

- Click the up or down arrow on the vertical scroll bar to scroll up and down within the object.

- Click the left or right arrow on the horizontal scroll bar to scroll left or right within the object.

Tip

If you prefer to have Access 2010 display database objects in the same manner that Windows 7 displays program windows (with maximize, minimize, and close buttons), click the File tab and then click Options. In the Access Options dialog box, display the Current Database tab. Then, in the Document Window Options section of the tab, select the Overlapping Windows option button and click OK.

Tab   Vertical scroll bar

Close button

Horizontal scroll bar

Closing a Database and Exiting Access 2010

When you finish working with an Access 2010 database, close it to free up system resources and let your computer run other programs more quickly. By the same token, after you complete all the work you need to do in Access 2010, you should exit the program entirely. If you work in a corporate environment or if your database contains sensitive information such as client addresses or account numbers, you should always close your database any time you walk away from your computer. Although it's unlikely that someone will wander by and copy or write down sensitive information, it's better that you make it as difficult as possible for anyone with bad intentions to make off with your data.

Close a Database

① Click the File tab.

② Click Close Database.

Exit Access 2010

① Click the File tab.

② Click Exit.

Tip

If you finish working with the current database and want to open another, save your work (if necessary), click the File tab, and then click Open.

Caution

Clicking the Close button at the top-right corner of the Access 2010 window will exit Access 2010, not just close the active database.

Displaying and Managing Database Objects

Access databases typically contain lots of objects: tables, where you store your data; forms, which enable you to enter data into tables quickly; queries, which enable you to extract subsets of data from your tables; and reports, which summarize your table data and query results. Access 2010 organizes your objects in the Navigation pane, found at the left edge of the program window. You can choose the order in which Access 2010 displays the objects and even choose whether to display a subset of your objects, but you always know where your objects are if you want them. The Shutter Bar, located at the top of the

Navigation pane, enables you to select how you want to view your database's objects. If you want to maximize the size of the object window, you can hide the Shutter Bar.

When you have more than one database object open, Access 2010 represents the objects as a series of tabs across the top of the database window. All you have to do to display an object is click its tab, and closing an object is as simple as clicking the Close button at the top-right corner of the object's window.

Open a Database Object

(1) If necessary, click the Shutter Bar Open/Close button to display the Navigation pane.

(2) Click the Shutter Bar.

(3) If there's no check mark next to All Access Objects, click All Access Objects.

(4) If necessary, click the Show Details button to display the objects in the desired category.

(5) Double-click the object you want to open.

Control Object Display in the Navigation Pane

① If necessary, click the Shutter Bar Open/Close Button to display the Navigation pane.

② Click the Shutter Bar.

③ Follow one of these steps:

- Select Tables and Related Views to display only your data tables and views.

- Select Object Type to display all the objects in your database, sorted by object type.

- Select Created Date to display all the objects in your database, sorted by the date the objects were created.

- Select Modified Date to display all the objects in your database, sorted by the date the objects were last changed.

Using the Access 2010 Help System

If you need to get help using Access 2010, there are a number of places you can look. One option is to right-click an object (such as a database object or a graphic) to see a list of things you can do with the object. You can also open the Access 2010 Help files and browse through them to find the answer to a specific question or just to explore.

Get Suggested Commands from Shortcut Menus

① Right-click any Access 2010 object to see the shortcut menu of commands.

② Click a command.

Get Microsoft Access 2010 Help

- Click the Microsoft Access Help button on the Ribbon.

Get Help on the Web

① Click the Microsoft Access Help button on the Ribbon.

② Click the Search button's down arrow and select where you want to look for help.

③ Type your search terms.

④ Click the Search button.

⑤ Browse the topics displayed for help and resources.

 Tip

You can visit the Microsoft Office Assistance Center site directly by opening your Web browser and typing *http://office.micro-soft.com/en-us/help/FX100485361033.aspx* in the Address box.

 Tip

If you use Access 2010 at work, you should definitely visit the Microsoft Office Online site at *http://office.microsoft.com/en-us/FX100647101033.aspx*. The Office Online site offers help files and product summaries, so you should have no trouble finding articles and demonstrations that can help you get your work done quickly.

4

Creating a Database

If none of the databases you can create using one of the Access 2010 database templates meets your needs, you can create a database and the tables it contains from scratch. When you choose to create a new table, you have complete control over the number of fields, the names of the fields, and what sort of data they can store. After you create the table, you can also add fields from the Field Templates task pane, which contains a wide variety of fields to store such data as times, dates, phone numbers, postal codes, names, addresses, and comments.

Once you create a table, whether in Design view or by using a template, you can change its structure as needed, such as renaming an existing field or adding an entirely new field to store additional data.

Designing a Database

The most basic object in a database is the table in which you store your data. You might be tempted to jam every type of data you want to store into a single table, but that's hardly ever the right way to design tables in a database. The following guidelines will help you create efficient tables.

One Table per Object

The first rule in creating database tables is to ensure that every table stores data about one type of object, whether that object is a person, a product, or an order. As an example, consider the Suppliers table from the Northwind sample database.

This table has a field for everything you want to know about a supplier, with nothing extra. Consider this alternative design, which adds fields to describe the supplier's products.

Aside from repeated data, deleting the record representing the last product from a supplier removes all information about that supplier from your database. Rather than risk losing that information, it is much more efficient to create one table for the suppliers and another for the products.

ID field

Give Every Table a Primary Key

Another important consideration in creating a table is to assign a *primary key*. This field contains a value that sets a record apart from all other records in the table. In the Northwind database's Shippers table, that role is filled by the ID field.

It's also possible to create a primary key made up of more than one field, as in the table shown in the following illustration. (Please note that this table is just a sample; it isn't in the Northwind database.)

The ProductID field identifies the product and the SupplierID field identifies the product's supplier. Because you can order the same product from more than one supplier, both the ProductID and SupplierID fields are needed to distinguish a record from all other records in the table.

Include Foreign Keys

A final thing you can do to make your tables more efficient is to include primary key fields from other tables, as with the SupplierIDs field in the Products table.

When a primary key from one table is stored in another table, it is called a *foreign key*. As you see later in this chapter, you can use foreign keys to create relationships between tables.

Viewing a Sample Database

One of the best ways to get a feel for using Access is to work with an existing database. The Northwind database, which you install along with Access, is a complete database with tables, queries, reports, and forms you can examine to see what goes into a solid database design.

Open a Sample Database

1. Start Access 2010.
2. Click Sample Templates.
3. Click Northwind.
4. Click Create.

Tip

The Northwind database contains a form that appears when you open the database. The form enables you to log in using different user accounts. If a database you create doesn't include accounts for individual users, that form won't appear.

Creating a New Database

If you want to create a new database from scratch, you can do so by creating a blank database and then adding your own tables and other objects. You can also create a new database based on an existing database, saving yourself lots of time and effort.

Begin a New Database

1. Click the File tab.

2. Click New.

3. Click Blank Database.

4. Type a name for your database.

5. Click the folder icon.

6. Navigate to the folder where you want to store the database.

7. Click OK.

8. Click Create.

Create a New Database Based on Another Database

(1) Open the database you want to use as a model and then click the File tab.

(2) Click Save Database As.

(3) Navigate to the directory where you want to save the new database.

(4) Type a different name for the new database.

(5) Click Save.

Caution

If you don't type a new name for your database, you will just save the existing database, not create a new file.

Creating Databases Using Database Templates

The Microsoft Access product team has one primary goal: to make it as easy as possible for you to create powerful and useful databases that help you get your work done quickly. You must have a great database program to meet that goal, but it also helps if the developers draw on the rest of the Microsoft community to design databases you can use without modification (for tasks such as tracking your contacts, sales, or workouts) or to use as the basis for your own custom databases. You can find those preexisting databases, called templates, installed on your computer and also on the Office.com Web site.

Create a Database from a Template

① If necessary, click the File tab and then choose Close Database to close any open database.

② Click a Template Category.

③ Click the desired template.

④ Type a name for your database.

⑤ Click Create.

Tip

You can select the folder where you want to save your database file by clicking the folder icon next to the File Name box in Backstage view.

Find Database Templates Online

1. If necessary, click the File tab and then click Close Database to close any open database.

2. Click an Office.com template category.

3. Click the desired template.

4. Type a name for your database.

5. Click Create.

Tip

You can search for templates on the Office.com Web site by typing one or more keywords in the Search Office.com For Templates box and clicking the Start Searching button.

Creating a New Table in Design View

After you plan your database, you can start creating tables to store your data. One good way to define your table's structure is to start out in Design view. When you look at a table in Design view, you can define the name of a field, select the type of data to go into that field (numerical values, currency values, text, dates, phone numbers, and so on), and write a description for that field. Field descriptions are one of the most overlooked parts of database design. It's easy to overlook them or see

them as unnecessary, but the reality is that you might forget what sort of data is supposed to go into a field. You could also leave the company and force someone else to figure out what a particular field should contain. If you've ever been handed someone else's database, you probably encountered a field you weren't sure about. Please make everyone's job easier by adding a description!

Create a Table in Design View

1 Click the Create tab.

2 In the Tables group, click Table Design.

3 Type a name for the first field and press Tab.

4 Click the Data Type down arrow.

Caution

Creating a database table that doesn't include a primary key field makes it difficult to get data out of your table by using queries and in relationships with other tables. You should always have a primary key field in every table you create.

5 Select a data type.

6 Type a description for the field.

7 Press Tab and repeat steps 4 through 7 to add fields.

8 Click the Save button.

9 Type a name for the table.

10 Click OK.

11 When asked whether you want Access 2010 to assign a primary key to your table, follow one of these steps:

- Click Yes to have Access 2010 assign a primary key.

- Click No to have Access 2010 create the table without a primary key.

- Click Cancel to continue without saving your table.

12 Click the Close box for the table.

Creating a New Table by Typing

It might seem strange to want to enter data into a table without first defining the table's structure, but there's one scenario where it makes perfect sense: when you're in a hurry and you have to get the data into the database quickly. When you type data into a blank table, Access 2010 assigns generic names to the fields, such as Field1, Field2, and so on. After the data's in the table, you can open the table in Design view and name the fields, define data types, and so on.

Create a New Table by Typing

① Click the Create tab.

② In the Tables group, click Table.

③ Type the data for the first new field and press Tab.

④ Repeat step 3 until you have typed all the data for one record, and then press Enter twice to return to the first field.

⑤ Click Save.

⑥ Type a name for your table.

⑦ Click OK.

⑧ Click the Close box for the table.

Tip

When you create a field by typing, Access 2010 defines the table's first field as a sequentially numbered field named ID, which serves as the table's primary key field. It's a good idea to leave the field in the table, but you should rename it to something more descriptive so you can identify it if you use it as a foreign key. If the table's name is Warehouses, for example, you could name the field **WarehouseID**.

Creating a New Table Using a Template

Rather than force you to create a new table from scratch when you start a new database, Access 2010 provides a number of templates you can use to create commonly used fields and tables quickly. When you display a table in Datasheet view, the Fields contextual tab on the Ribbon displays buttons you can use to add the five basic field types: text, number, currency, date & time, and yes/no. You can select from more built-in field types, or insert a set of multiple related fields by clicking the More Fields button and clicking the desired option from the menu that appears.

Add Fields from the Add & Delete Ribbon Group

1 Open a table in Datasheet view.

2 In the table, click a cell in the Click to Add column.

3 Click the Fields contextual tab.

4 Click the type of field you want to add.

Add More Types of Fields

① Open a table in Datasheet view.

② In the table, click a cell in the Click to Add column.

③ Click the Fields contextual tab.

④ Click More Fields.

⑤ Click the type of field you want to add.

Add Multiple Related Fields at One Time

① Open a table in Datasheet view.

② In the table, click a cell in the Click to Add column.

③ Click the Fields contextual tab.

④ Click More Fields.

⑤ In the Quick Start section of the list, click the set of fields you want to add.

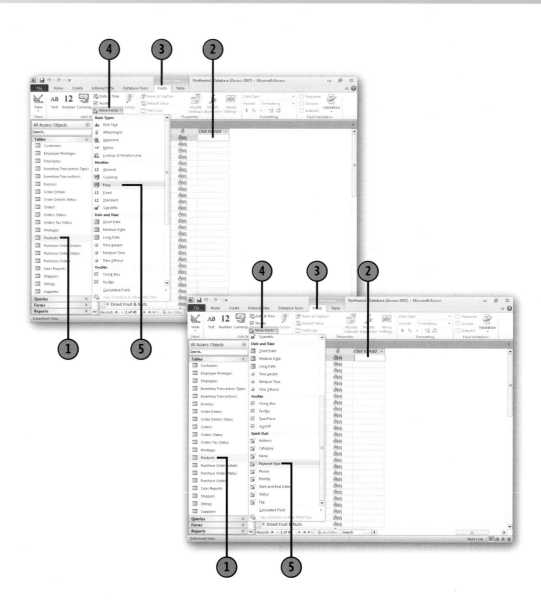

Creating a New Table Using Application Parts

Access 2010 enables you to create databases and fields using templates. One new capability in Access 2010, Application Parts, enables you to create a table and several related forms, queries, and reports that display and summarize the data from that table. For example, if you want to maintain a list of contacts, you can use the Access 2010 Contacts Application Part to create a Contacts table, three forms, a query, and four reports to view your contacts, display a phone list, and create address labels based on that information.

Create a Table, Forms, and Reports Using Application Parts

1. Click the Create tab.

2. Click Application Parts.

3. Click the Application Part you want to use.

4. Select the There Is No Relationship option.

5. Click Create.

Tip

If the Application Part you used relates to an existing table in your database, such as if your Contacts table tracks your contacts with the individuals named in your Customers table, you can use the Create Relationship Wizard to define that relationship.

Setting a Primary Key

One aspect of sound table design is to have a field (or group of fields) with a value unique to each row in the table. The fields that have the unique value are called the *primary key* field(s). Because each row's primary key field (or fields) contains a unique value, Access 2010 can distinguish each row from all the other rows in the table. Why is that important? Consider what would happen if a store used your phone number to identify you when you called in to place an order. If you change phone numbers and the next person assigned your phone number calls in before you do, the store replaces your information with the new caller's, potentially wiping out any record you had of doing business with the store.

Assign a Primary Key

1. Display the tables in your database.

2. Right-click the desired table.

3. Click Design View.

4. Click any cell in the row representing the field to be the primary key.

5. Make sure the Design tab is displayed, and click the Primary Key button.

6. Click the Save button to save your work.

7. Click the Close box.

Tip

The primary key shouldn't contain meaningful information. The best value for a primary key field is a number that Access 2010 increments for each row in a table. That type of field is called an AutoNumber field.

Tip

You can create a multiple-field primary key by Ctrl-clicking the row selectors of the fields you want to include in the primary key.

Getting Data from Other Access 2010 Tables

Many times you find that data from another database would be nice to have in the database you're working on. You can bring tables (or other objects) into your database using the controls on the External Data tab. Copying tables from another database enables you to use the data as it exists at the time you make the copy, so any updates you make to the original table are not reflected in the copy, and vice versa. If you want to copy the structure of the table and not the data, you can do so easily.

Copy a Table from Another Database

1. Click the External Data tab.
2. Click Access.
3. Click Browse.
4. Double-click the database from which you want to import the table.

Tip

After you click OK, you might be able to save the import operation you just created. If you want to save your import so you can repeat it later, select the Save Import Steps check box, type a name for the import operation, type a description for the import operation (if desired), and then click Save Import.

(5) Select the Import Tables, Queries, Forms, Reports, Macros, and Modules into the Current Database option.

(6) Click OK.

(7) Click the table or tables to import.

(8) Click Options.

(9) Follow either of these steps:

- Select the Definition and Data option to copy the table structure and data.

- Select the Definition Only option to copy just the table structure.

(10) Click OK.

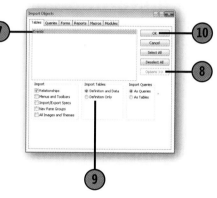

Tip

You can import data from other types of database objects by clicking the object type (for example, Queries) in the Import Objects dialog box and then clicking the object from which you want to get your data.

See Also

For information on linking to a table instead of copying it, see "Linking to a Table in Another Access 2010 Database" on page 196.

Tip

If you clicked a table to include it in the list of tables to be imported, but have changed your mind, you can click the table again to deselect it.

Relationships Explained

One-to-Many Relationships

One of the strengths of Access is the ability to create relationships between tables. As an example of a relationship, consider the Customers and Orders tables from the Northwind sample database.

In the Northwind business case, every order comes from a single customer. Of course, a customer can place more than one order, which means that the Customers and Orders tables are in a one-to-many relationship with the Customers table on the "one" side and the Orders table on the "many" side.

Many-to-Many Relationships

It is also possible for two tables to be in a *many-to-many* relationship, where multiple records from one table relate to multiple records from another table. As an example, consider the Products and Orders tables in the Northwind database: A product can be included in many orders, and an order can include many products. The problem is that you can't relate the two tables directly without adding fields to the Orders table to hold spots for more than one item, as in the following incorrect example.

This table is poorly designed because it forces you to enter data about the customer and the order in each record, instead of just once, and an order can't be for more items than you have spots in the table. The proper way to manage the relationship is to create a *transition table*, which bridges the gap between the Products and Orders tables. In the Northwind database, the Order Details table is a transition table.

The Order Details table is on the "many" side of two one-to-many relationships—the first with the Products table, and the second with the Orders table. By bridging the two tables, it lets you manage the relationship between the Orders and Products tables without resorting to improper table design.

Creating Relationships Between Tables

When the primary key from one table is present in another table, you can create a relationship between the two tables. This ability to link two (or more) tables together is one reason why relational databases are so powerful: You make your data easier to read by creating simple tables and then use your computer's processing power to combine tables of data into useful information you can use to make business decisions.

Define a Relationship

1. Click the Database Tools tab.

2. Click Relationships.

3. If one or more of the tables you want to relate doesn't appear in the Relationships window, click the Show Table button.

4. Click the first table to add to the Relationships window.

5. Click Add.

6. Repeat steps 4 and 5 as necessary.

7. When you finish adding tables, click Close.

Tip

To delete a table from the Relationships window, right-click the table's title bar and then click Hide Table.

8 Drag the primary key field from the first table to the corresponding foreign key field in the second table.

9 Click Create.

10 Click the Close button to close the Relationships window.

Tip

The foreign key and primary key fields don't have to have the same name in each table; they just need to denote the same data.

Caution

It is possible to add a table more than once: make sure you click the name of the table you want to add! Nothing bad happens, but you won't have added the tables you want to work with.

Enforcing Referential Integrity

When you create a relationship between two tables, you need to make sure that data in the two tables remains consistent. If you no longer order from a supplier, you would want all products from that supplier deleted from the Products table when you delete the supplier's data from the Suppliers table. Enforcing referential integrity lets you do that.

Enforce Referential Integrity

① Click the Database Tools tab.

② Click Relationships.

③ Double-click the line representing the relationship you want to edit.

④ Select the Enforce Referential Integrity
check box.

- Selecting the Cascade Update Related
  Fields check box means Access 2010 will
  change the values in foreign key fields
  when the corresponding primary key
  field's value is changed.

- Selecting the Cascade Delete Related
  Records check box means that deleting
  a record from the primary field in a relationship will cause Access 2010 to delete
  all related records in the second table.

⑤ Click OK.

⑥ Click the Save button.

⑦ Click the Close box of the Relationships
window.

5

Customizing Fields

When you create a database table using a wizard, Microsoft Access 2010 assigns a data type and properties to each field in the table. When you create a table from scratch or if you want to modify the settings Access 2010 applied to the table, you can change a field's properties so it stores data efficiently and interacts well with other fields in the database. Access 2010 also gives you several ways to facilitate accurate data entry. When you and your colleagues need to enter data such as phone numbers or postal codes, you can define an input mask that visually indicates the data pattern required for that field. If a field often contains the same value, you can set that value as the default. And when there are only a few possible values for a field, such as when you need to select a category from your company's list of product categories, you can create a lookup list from which to choose the appropriate value or values. Finally, you can enable your colleagues to attach files, such as customer faxes, to a record; or create a memo field that enables users to add their own comments without being able to edit or delete existing comments.

Working with Tables

It's easy to create tables in Access 2010, but you're not stuck with the first version of the table. After you create a table, you can modify it by adding, deleting, and reordering fields. While the order of your fields doesn't affect how your table functions within the database, changing the fields' order can make it easier for you and your colleagues to understand your table's structure when you view the table's data in Datasheet view and structure in Design view. In addition to the instructions to modify your table, this section includes a table that describes the data types available to you in Access 2010.

Delete a Field

1. Open a table in Design view.

2. Click the row selector of the row you want to delete.

3. Click the Delete Rows button.

4. Click Yes to confirm that you want to delete the row.

Caution

Deleting a primary key field prevents you from distinguishing a table row from other table rows or relating the table to other tables in your database.

Tip

If you add a field to a table that already contains data, remember to set aside time to fill in the new data for any existing records.

Caution

Deleting a field gets rid of all the data in that field—it can't be retrieved. You should strongly consider making a backup copy of a table when you make a significant change such as deleting a field.

Add a Field

1. Open a table in Design view.

2. Click the row selector of the row below where you want the new field to appear.

3. Click the Insert Rows button.

4. Type a name for the new field.

5. Assign a data type.

Arrange Fields

1. Open a table in Design view.

2. Click the row selector of the row you want to move.

3. Drag the row selector to the new position. A line appears to show where the row will be moved in the table.

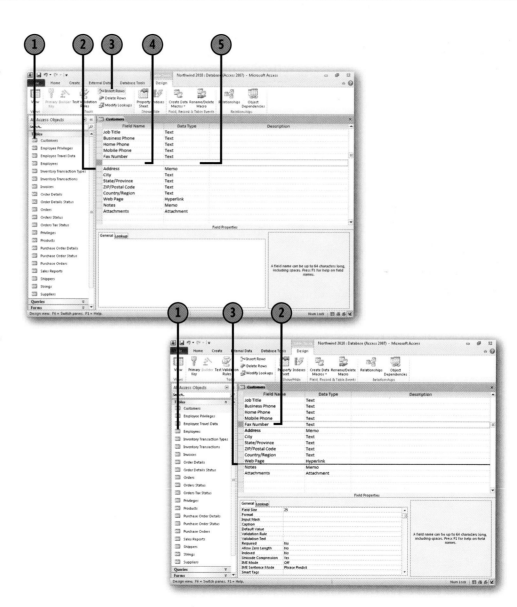

Assigning a Data Type

In Access 2010, some operations such as arithmetic or date comparisons require you to assign the proper data type to a field. You have a number of data types to choose from, depending on your needs. For example, creating an AutoNumber field directs Access 2010 to add a sequential value to a table row automatically, which is useful for distinguishing a particular table row from all other rows in the table. Creating a memo field gives you and your colleagues a place to type notes about a table record, making it possible for information workers to add details as to why they entered data in a certain way or to add customer comments.

Pick a Data Type

1. Open a table in Design view.

2. Click in the Data Type box of the field you want to edit.

3. Click the down arrow.

4. Click the data type to assign to the field.

Available Data Types

Data Type	Description
Text	A series of numbers and letters of up to 255 characters.
Memo	Same as the Text data type, with an upper limit of 64,000 characters.
Number	Numeric data.
Date/Time	Dates and times between the years 100 and 9999.
Currency	Primarily monetary amounts, but can also be used to set a specific number of digits to the right of the decimal point.
AutoNumber	A unique number for each row, either one greater than the value in the most recently created row or a random value.
Yes/No	A Yes/No, On/Off, or True/False value.
OLE Object	A link to another file, such as a Microsoft Word document.
Hyperlink	A link that opens a file, a location in a file, or a Web address.
Calculated	Results of a calculation. The calculation must refer to other fields in the same table. You use the Expression Builder to create the calculation.
Lookup	A list of values derived from either an existing table (or query) field or from a list you enter directly; you can choose to allow users to assign multiple values to the field.
Attachment	A file, or set of files, included as part of the record.

Viewing or Changing Field Properties

Every field has a number of properties, such as the maximum number of characters allowed in the field. Setting a field's properties helps control the type of data entered into the field, which makes it less likely that your colleagues will enter erroneous data. The properties available to you are different for each data type, but you can view all the available properties in the Field Properties pane, which appears at the bottom of the screen when you open a table in Design view.

View Field Properties

1. Open a table in Design view.

2. Click within the row representing the field with the properties you want to change.

3. Click the name of the property you want to change.

4. Follow any of these steps:

   - Type a new value for the property.

   - Click the down arrow, and choose a new value from the list.

   - Click the Build button to open the Expression Builder.

Introducing the Expression Builder

When you set a validation rule to check field data or when you create a calculation to find the total value of an order, you create an expression to evaluate the contents of one or more table fields. Rather than make you memorize how to identify the fields you want to use or which operators are available, you can use the controls in the Expression Builder to create your expressions quickly.

The expression appears here

Click OK when you've created your expression

Double-click to see categories of available functions

Double-click to see functions within a category

Click to see a list of available constants

Click to see a list of available operators

Click Help to get more help using the Expression Builder

The available items for a group (or subgroup) appear here

Click a subgroup to narrow the list of functions, constants, or operators displayed

Formatting Field Contents

Access 2010 lets you choose how to display the contents of data in your tables. For example, you can display the field's contents in all upper- or lowercase letters, change the color of the text, or display characters in addition to the data entered into the field. For example, if a product is only available by the case, adding the word "cases" after the number would remove any confusion as to the quantity being ordered. Adding formatting instructions only changes how data is displayed—it doesn't affect the data itself.

Change Field Format

1 Open a table in Design view.

2 Click the name of the field to format.

3 Type the formatting instructions in the Format property box.

Tip

A down arrow appears in the Format property box when the box is active; clicking the down arrow displays a list of recently used formats. To reuse a format, simply click it.

Character	Resulting Format
!	Left align.
<	Lowercase.
>	Uppercase.
&	Instruction to follow.
"Text"	Display the text as it appears between the quotes. &" kg" displays the value "16" as "16 kg."
(space)	Insert a blank space.
\	Display the next character as entered. **&\m** displays the text "100" as "100m."
@	Require a character; **@@@-@@@@** displays the text "5550011" as "555-0101."
*	Fill all blank spaces in the field with the named character. In a field with a maximum character property of eight, **&*#** displays "five" as "five####."
[color]	Display the field's contents in one of the eight available named colors (black, blue, green, cyan, red, magenta, yellow, and white).

Creating Input Masks

Databases are only as good as the data they hold, so it's important that you and your colleagues enter data correctly. You can guide data entry in text and date fields by creating an input mask, which gives you a template to follow when entering data in a field. For example, if your company's product codes follow a particular pattern, you can establish that pattern by using an input mask, ensuring that you and your colleagues enter the right sort of data into the field.

Define an Input Mask

1. Open a table in Design view.

2. Click the field for which you want to create the input mask.

3. Click in the Input Mask property box.

4. Click the Build button.

5. Click Yes to save the table.

6. Click the desired input mask.

7. Type values in the Try It box to ensure that the input mask works as expected.

8. Click Next.

9. To choose a new placeholder character, click the Placeholder down arrow and then click the new character.

10. Click Next.

11. Select the option indicating whether you want to store the data as entered or with the characters in the input mask.

12. Click Finish.

Tip

Assign the Text data type to fields holding phone numbers so that you can take advantage of the Phone Number input mask.

Tip

If the data entered into a field is sensitive and shouldn't be read by someone watching as you or your colleague enters the data, choose the Password input mask.

Edit an Input Mask

① Click the field to which you assigned an input mask.

② Click in the Input Mask property box.

③ Change the input mask using the available symbols.

Symbol	Description
0	Required digit (0 to 9)
9	Optional digit (0 to 9)
#	Any digit or space
L	Required letter
?	Optional letter
>	Makes following characters uppercase
<	Makes following characters lowercase
A	Required alphanumeric character
a	Optional alphanumeric character
&	Requires any character or space
C	Optional character or space

Tip

You can also reopen the Input Mask Wizard by clicking the Build button at the right edge of the Input Mask property box.

Assigning Required Fields and Requiring Data Entry

Some data is more important than other data. For example, a salesperson might need to know a contact's phone number, but not necessarily the contact's address. You can tell Access 2010 to prevent someone from moving beyond a required field without entering a value. For text and memo fields, you can require users to enter at least one character of text.

Require Data Entry

1. Open a table in Design view.

2. Click the field for which you want to require data entry.

3. Click in the Required property box.

4. Click the down arrow.

5. Click Yes.

Disallow Zero-Length Strings

1. Open a table in Design view.

2. Click the text or memo field for which you want to require the user to enter at least one character of text.

3. Click in the Allow Zero Length property box.

4. Click the down arrow.

5. Click No.

Setting Default Values

When you enter data, you often find that you enter the same value in a field many times. For example, most of your customers might come from the United States, but you have a Country field for those customers outside the United States. Setting a default value for a field saves you the trouble of entering the expected data over and over while still allowing you to edit the value if needed.

Assign a Default Value

① Open a table in Design view.

② Click the field to which you want to assign the default value.

③ Type the default value in the Default Value box.

Tip

As your needs change, you should periodically review any default values you've set to be sure you aren't slowing yourself down by deleting incorrect data.

Indexing Field Values

When you create an index of a field's values, Access 2010 maintains an internal record of the values in a field, which the program can then use to find table records with specific values.

Access 2010 always keeps an index of a table's primary key field's values.

Create an Index

1. Open a table in Design view.

2. Click the field to index.

3. Click the Indexed property name.

4. Click the Indexed down arrow.

5. Click either Yes (Duplicates OK) or Yes (No Duplicates).

Try This!

Open the Northwind sample database, click Tables on the Objects bar, double-click Products, and then click Design. Click any cell in the ProductName row of the design grid, and then click Indexed in the Field Properties section. Click the down arrow that appears and then click Yes (No Duplicates). This change requires every new product entered into the table to have a unique name. This specific change works for Northwind, which carries unique products, but may not work for a business that buys common items from more than one supplier.

Tip

Indexes work best in fields with lots of different values. In large tables, indexing the values in commonly used fields lets Access 2010 find what you're looking for quickly.

Caution

Access 2010 updates all its indexes every time you add or update a table record. Creating unneeded indexes can greatly slow down data entry, especially on older systems.

Validating Data Entry

Some categories of data, such as credit limits or the date someone joined a club, have to meet certain criteria. You can make sure data entered into fields meets those criteria (for example, all credit limits are $5,000 or less) by performing data validation. When a user tries to enter data that isn't appropriate for the field, you can display a message letting the user know what went wrong.

Perform Data Validation

1. Open a table in Design view.

2. Click the field for which you want to validate data entry.

3. Click Validation Rule.

4. Click the Build button.

5. Create the validation rule in the Expression Builder.

6. Click OK.

Set Validation Text

1. Open a table in Design view.

2. Click the field to which you want to assign validation text.

3. Type your validation text in the Validation Text box.

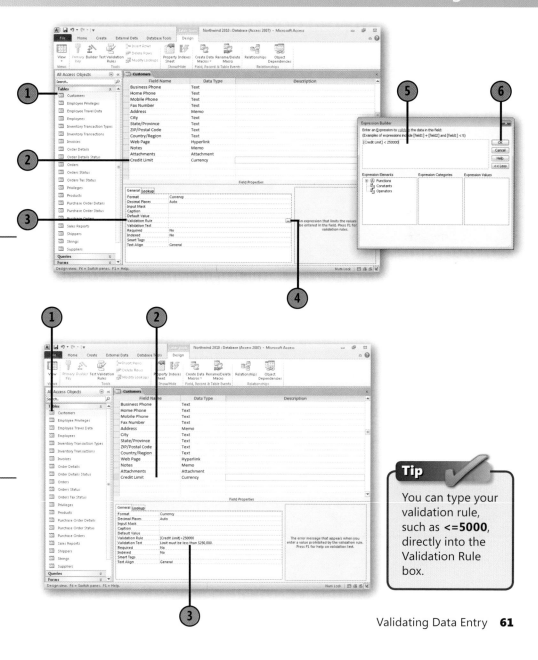

Tip

You can type your validation rule, such as **<=5000**, directly into the Validation Rule box.

Creating a Lookup Field

Many times the data you need to enter in one table can be found in another table. In the Northwind database, for example, if you add a new product, you must assign it to a category. Rather than make you open the Categories table separately and find the value you need, Access 2010 lets you display those values in a list. You can also create your own list rather than drawing values from an existing source.

Define a Field as a Lookup Field

① Open a table in Design view.

② Click the field to define as a lookup field.

③ Click the Data Type cell, click the down arrow, and then click Lookup Wizard.

④ Select the I Want the Lookup Field to Get the Values from Another Table or Query option.

⑤ Click Next.

Tip

You should strongly consider using lookup fields where spelling errors of even a single letter can throw off your data.

6 Click the table or query to provide the values.

7 Click Next.

8 Click the first field to provide the values.

9 Click the Add button.

10 Repeat steps 6 and 7 to add more fields.

11 Click Next.

12 Click the first sorting field's down arrow.

13 Click the name of the field by which you want to sort the values of the lookup column.

14 Click the sorting order button to toggle between Ascending and Descending order.

15 Click Next.

16 Click Finish.

Tip

Leave the Hide key column check box selected so the person using the lookup column sees only the values in the field you want him or her to see, not the values in the primary key field.

Allow Multiple Selections from a Lookup Field

① Open a table in Design view.

② Click the field to define as a lookup field.

③ Click the Data Type cell, click the down arrow, and then click Lookup Wizard.

④ Select the I Want the Lookup Field to Get the Values from Another Table or Query option.

⑤ Click Next.

⑥ Click the table or query to provide the values.

⑦ Click Next.

⑧ Click the first field to provide the values.

⑨ Click Add.

⑩ Click Next three times.

⑪ Select the Allow Multiple Values check box.

⑫ Click Finish.

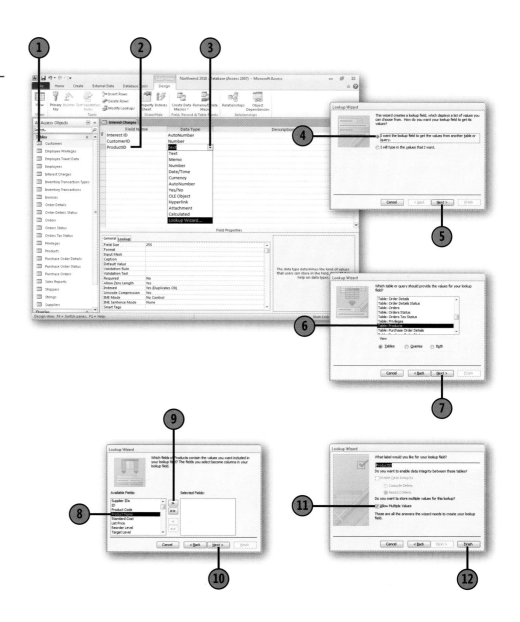

Draw Lookup Values from a Data List

①　Open a table in Design view.

②　Click the field to define as a lookup field.

③　Click the Data Type cell, click the down arrow, and then click Lookup Wizard.

④　Select the I Will Type In The Values That I Want option.

⑤　Click Next.

⑥　Type the number of columns you want in your lookup list.

⑦　Type the first row of values in the list and then press Tab.

⑧　Continue adding rows until all values are in the list.

⑨　Click Finish.

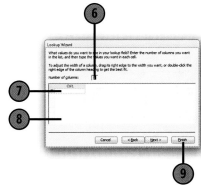

Creating an Append-Only Memo Field

Most database table fields contain dry, factual data such as prices, quantities, and descriptions. You can extend the facts in your tables by creating memo fields, which can contain up to 64,000 characters. Memo fields are ideal for storing comments about database records, but you might not want to allow users to delete existing comments. To allow users to add but not delete comments to a memo field, you can make the memo field an append-only field.

Create an Append-Only Field

1. Open a table in Design view.
2. Click the field to define as an append-only field.
3. Click the Data Type cell.
4. Click the down arrow.
5. Click Memo.
6. Click the Append Only property.
7. Click the down arrow.
8. Click Yes.

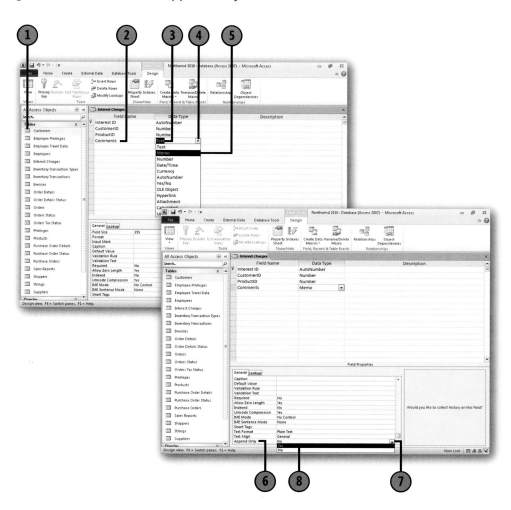

Creating an Attachment Field

Databases can contain information about business transactions, but there's a lot more to business than simple numerical and text values. If you work with paper invoices, purchase orders, or correspondence, you can scan those documents into electronic form and attach the documents to the record to which the documents are related. Alternatively, if you have another file (such as a Word document, product image, or Excel workbook) that's related to the item described by the record, you can also attach those files to the record.

Create an Attachment Field

1. Open a table in Design view.

2. Click the field to define as an attachment field.

3. Click the Data Type cell.

4. Click the down arrow.

5. Click Attachment.

6

Customizing Tables

In section 5, I explained how to change a table's structure by working with the table in Design view. This section shows you how to work with a table in Datasheet view, in which the table data is displayed in a worksheet where each column represents a table field and each row represents a table record. Changing how your data is displayed in Datasheet view can make your table easier to read and work with—for example, you might change the order of fields in a table to reflect the natural order you and your colleagues follow when entering data from a paper form into the table. In this section, you will learn how to manipulate table columns and rows, find and replace text, enter data using AutoCorrect, view a subworksheet, and filter table records.

Finding and Replacing Text

After you enter data into a table, you might need to search the table for a particular word; or if one of your suppliers changes the name of a product, you might need to replace some or all instances of a word or phrase. You can do that using the Find and Replace tools in Microsoft Access 2010. But be careful when you replace text! If you replace every occurrence of the word *chip* with the word *crisp*, you could end up selling *chocolate crisp cookies.*

Find Text

① Open a table in Datasheet view.

② Click the Home tab.

③ Click Find.

④ Type the text you want to find in the Find What field.

⑤ Click the Look In down arrow, and click the field or table where you expect to find the text.

⑥ Click the Match down arrow and then choose one of these options:

- Click Whole Field to return table records where your text matches the entire contents of a field.

- Click Any Part Of Field to return table records where your text is found within a field.

- Click Start Of Field to return table records where your text is found at the beginning of a field.

⑦ Click Find Next.

Replace Text

1. Open a table in Datasheet view.

2. Click the Home tab.

3. Click Replace.

4. Type the text you want to replace in the Find What box.

5. Type the text to substitute for the original text in the Replace With box.

6. Click the Look In down arrow, and click the field or table where you expect to find the text.

7. Click the Match down arrow and then choose one of these options:

   • Click Whole Field to return table records where your text matches the entire contents of a field.

   • Click Any Part Of Field to return table records where your text is found within a field.

   • Click Start Of Field to return table records where your text is found at the beginning of a field.

8. Click Find Next to locate the first instance of the text to be replaced.

9. Click Replace.

Entering Data Using AutoCorrect

When you enter data into a table, Access 2010 examines what you type and corrects any common spelling errors it knows about. You can also add your own AutoCorrect values to streamline data entry—for example, you could have Access 2010 recognize the abbreviation *sarsp* and replace it with

sarsaparilla. If you find that Access 2010 insists on changing a text entry that you know is correct, you can delete a particular AutoCorrect entry. As an example, one of your projects might have the code name AMDE, which Access 2010 automatically changes to MADE.

Add Text with AutoCorrect

1 Open a table in Datasheet view.

2 Begin typing text in a cell.

3 When a value AutoCorrect recognizes appears, the program replaces the incorrect value with the correct value.

Tip

To undo an AutoCorrect change, press Ctrl+Z.

Turn AutoCorrect On or Off

① Click the File tab.

② Click Options.

③ Click Proofing.

④ Click AutoCorrect Options.

⑤ Do either of the following:

- Select the Replace Text As You Type check box to turn on AutoCorrect.

- Deselect the Replace Text As You Type check box to turn off AutoCorrect.

⑥ Click OK.

⑦ Click OK.

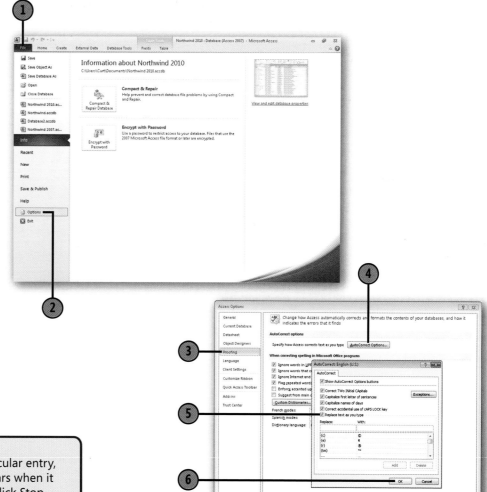

Tip

If you want to have Access 2010 *not* correct a particular entry, click the AutoCorrect Options smart tag that appears when it makes a correction. From the menu that appears, click Stop Automatically Correcting *"entry"*. Clicking Change Back to *"entry"* from the AutoCorrect Options smart tag's list undoes this change without deleting the rule.

Add AutoCorrect Values

(1) Click the File tab.

(2) Click Options.

(3) Click Proofing.

(4) Click AutoCorrect Options.

(5) Type the text to be replaced in the Replace box.

(6) Type the text to substitute for the entered text in the With box.

(7) Click Add.

(8) Click OK.

(9) Click OK.

Try This!

Click the File tab and then click Options. Click Proofing and then type *sarsp* in the Replace box, type *sarsaparilla* in the With box, and click Add. Click OK to close the AutoCorrect dialog box. Now every time you type *sarsp*, AutoCorrect replaces it with *sarsaparilla*.

Adding and Editing Text

Once you open a table, you can edit the existing data, add new data, or copy data from one cell and paste it into another. You can edit text using the same techniques that you use in other Microsoft Office 2010 applications. When you cut or copy table data, the Office Clipboard keeps track of the last 24 items you cut or copy. If you want Access 2010 to undo the last change you made, you can do so by pressing Ctrl+Z or by clicking the Undo button on the Quick Access Toolbar.

Select Text

- Move the mouse pointer over a cell until the pointer turns into a white cross and then click in the cell.

- Double-click a word to select it.

- Drag the mouse pointer over text to select it.

Delete Text

- Click to the right of the text to be deleted and press Backspace to delete it one character at a time.

- Select the text and press Delete.

Undoing Operations

- To undo an operation, click the Undo button in the Quick Access Toolbar.

Undo button   Select text using the mouse

Copy and Paste Text

① Select the text you want to copy.

② Click the Home tab.

③ Click the Copy button.

④ Click the position where you want to paste the text.

⑤ Click the Paste button.

Copy and Paste Items with the Office Clipboard

① On the Home tab, click the Clipboard group's dialog box launcher.

② Select the contents of a cell and click Copy.

③ Click the cell where you want to paste the contents.

④ Click the item to be pasted.

Tip

You can remove an item from the Clipboard by displaying the Clipboard and then hovering your mouse pointer over the item. Click the down arrow that appears and then click Delete. To delete every item in the Clipboard, display the Clipboard and then click the Clear All button at the top of the Clipboard task pane.

Manipulating Columns

You can change how data is displayed in your worksheet by changing the order of the table's columns. You can also add or delete fields by inserting a column (which creates a new field) or deleting a column (which deletes the field it represents). If you want to copy the contents of a column to another table, or even to another Office document, you can do so easily.

Relocate a Column

① Click the column head of the column you want to move.

② Drag the column to its new position in the worksheet. A vertical black line appears on the edge between the two columns where the moved column will be pasted.

Caution

Be sure to release the mouse button after you click the column head; if you don't, you'll select more than one column instead of moving only the column you want to move.

Insert a Column

① Right-click the column head of the column to the right of where you want the new column to appear.

② Choose Insert Field from the shortcut menu.

Rename a Column

① Right-click the column head of the column.

② Choose Rename Field from the shortcut menu.

③ Type a new name for the column and press Enter.

Copy a Column

① Right-click the column head of the column you want to copy.

② Choose Copy from the shortcut menu.

③ Click the column head of a blank column.

④ Click the Paste button.

Modifying Columns and Rows

The standard height of worksheet rows is just enough to display the contents of a row. While that setting fits a lot of data on a sheet, it doesn't always make it easy to read the row's contents. You can increase the height of your table's rows or change the width of individual columns to show more or less of the row or column's contents. Bear in mind that you can't change the height of individual rows; changes you make to one row affect every row in your table.

Change Row Height

① Move the mouse pointer over an edge of a row selector.

② Drag the edge up or down.

> **Tip**
>
> To change the width of more than one column, select the columns to change, move the mouse pointer over the edge of any of those columns' selectors, and drag the edge to the desired width. Every selected column takes on the new setting.

Change Column Width

① Move the mouse pointer over an edge of the column selector of the column you want to resize.

② Drag the edge to the left or right.

Viewing a Subworksheet

When two tables are in a one-to-many relationship, you can create a subworksheet that displays records from the table on the "many" side of the relationship. A plus sign appears next to the key field of the worksheet on the "one" side of the relationship, indicating that a subworksheet is available. If your table doesn't have a subworksheet associated with it, you can set your table's properties to identify the table or query that you want to display as a subworksheet.

Open and Close a Subworksheet

1. Open a table in Datasheet view.

2. Click the plus sign next to the value for which you want to see records in the related subworksheet.

3. Click the minus sign to hide the subworksheet.

See Also

For more information about relationships, see "Creating Relationships between Tables" on page 44.

Create a Subworksheet

① Open a table in Design view.

② Click the Design tab.

③ Click Property Sheet.

④ Click the Subdatasheet Name property field, click the down arrow that appears and then click the table or query to provide data for the subworksheet.

⑤ If necessary, click the Link Child Fields down arrow and then click the name of the foreign key field in the table to provide data for the subworksheet.

⑥ Click the Close button to close the Property Sheet task pane.

Filtering Table Records

Often you will be interested in viewing only some of the records in a table. For example, you might want to find all your customers or suppliers from a particular state or country. You can narrow the records shown in a table by creating a filter that hides records not meeting your criteria. The records aren't erased, though; when you remove the filter, they display normally.

Filter Table Records

1. Open a table in Datasheet view.

2. Select the text to serve as the base for the filter.

3. Click the Home tab.

4. Click Selection.

5. Click the type of filter you want to create.

Filter by Form

① Open a table in Datasheet view.

② Click the Home tab.

③ Click Advanced.

④ Click Filter By Form.

⑤ Click the cell in the column by which you want to filter.

⑥ Click the down arrow that appears.

⑦ Select the value by which you want to filter.

⑧ Click the Toggle Filter button to apply the filter.

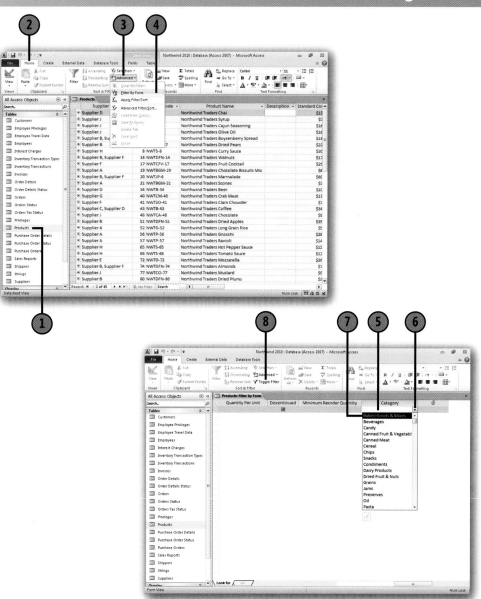

Remove a Filter

① Click the Home tab.

② Click Toggle Filter.

Filter Records by the Contents of More than One Column

1. Open a table in Datasheet view.

2. Click the Home tab.

3. Click Advanced.

4. Click Advanced Filter/Sort.

5. Click the down arrow in the first Field cell and then click the name of the field by which you want to filter.

6. Type the expression by which you want to filter the table.

7. Repeat steps 5 and 6 as needed to add other fields to the filter.

8. Click Toggle Filter.

Open the Northwind sample database and then open the Products table in Datasheet view. Click the Home tab, click Advanced, and then click Advanced Filter/Sort. Click in the first Field cell, click the down arrow that appears, and then click Category. In the Criteria cell of the first column, type **Bev-erages**. Click in the second column's Field cell, click the down arrow, and then click Standard Cost. Type **>10** in the second column's Criteria cell. In the Sort & Filter group on the ribbon, click Toggle Filter to display the filtered table. Click the Toggle Filter button again to remove the filter.

Tip

You can use the Expression Builder to create your filter by right-clicking in a Criteria cell and choosing the Build command from the submenu that appears.

7 Creating Forms

One of the nice things about Microsoft Access 2010 is that it makes it easy for you to view existing table data and even add new data using forms. A form is a database object that lets you enter and view table data without viewing the table in datasheet mode. Instead, you can create a form that spaces the data out on the page, limit the number of table fields displayed so that only the most important or relevant data is shown, and modify the form once you've created it to make the form easier to use.

Creating a Simple Form

Access makes it possible for you to create powerful and complex forms, but there will be plenty of occasions where a simple form that contains all the fields from a table will meet your needs. Creating a simple form is a straightforward process: You select the table from which you want to create your form, tell Access you want to create a simple form based on that table, and you're done. The whole process takes a maximum of four mouse clicks from start to finish.

Create a Simple Form

1. In the Navigation Pane, click a table.
2. Click the Create tab.
3. Click Form.

Creating a Form Using the Form Wizard

Access makes it easy for you to create forms based on the tables in your database. By using the Form Wizard, you can choose the data source, the type of form, and the form's appearance. The Form Wizard also includes a wide variety of form themes from which to choose, enabling you to create great-looking forms without doing any design work yourself.

Step Through the Form Wizard

① Click the Create tab.

② Click Form Wizard.

③ Click the Tables/Queries down arrow.

④ Click the table to provide the values and structure for the form.

⑤ Click a field in the Available Fields box and then click either of the following:

- Click Add to add the selected field.
- Click Add All to add all fields to the form.

⑥ Click Next.

⑦ Select the layout for the form.

⑧ Click Next.

⑨ Type a name for the form.

⑩ Click Finish.

Tip

You can remove a field from the Selected Fields box by clicking the field and then clicking Remove. Clicking Remove All clears the Selected Fields box.

Tip

You should create a sample form of each of the four main types (Columnar, Tabular, Justified, and Datasheet) to see which type will best meet your needs in a particular situation.

Creating a Form in Design View

If you'd rather not use the Form Wizard to create a form, you can open a blank form and manually add controls. If you want to add fields from a table to your form, you can display fields from existing tables by displaying the Field List task pane and dragging the desired fields to the body of the form.

Create a Form in Design View

1. Click the Create tab.

2. Click Form Design.

3. If necessary, click the Design contextual tab.

4. If necessary, click Property Sheet.

5. Click Data.

6. Click Record Source.

7. Click the down arrow.

8. Click the table from which you want to draw your values.

9 Click Add Existing Fields.

10 Drag fields from the Field List task pane to the body of the form.

11 Click Save.

12 Type a name for the form.

13 Click OK.

Try This!

Open the Northwind sample database, display the Navigation Pane, and then click the Products table. On the Create tab, in the Forms group, click Form Design. After the form appears, on the Design contextual tab, in the Tools group, click Property Sheet. In the Property Sheet task pane, click the Record Source property name, click the down arrow that appears, and then click Products. On the Design contextual tab, in the Tools group, click Add Existing Fields. Drag the ID and Product Name fields to the body of the form. Click the Save button on the Quick Access Toolbar, type ProductSample in the dialog box that appears, and then click OK.

Creating a Multiple Items Form

In general, you use forms for data entry and for viewing table or query records. For those tasks, many users prefer to view one record at a time. Typing a new record into an otherwise blank form limits the distractions caused by other data. The same can be said of viewing a table or query; if you want to see more than one record at a time, you could view the table or query in Datasheet view.

The problem with Datasheet view is that it presents a basic grid that, although it has gridlines, doesn't make it very easy to distinguish one record from another. If you want to present or enter your data while still viewing other records in the table or query, you can create a Multiple Items Form. This type of form displays your data in a grid layout, but you have much more control over the grid and the data's appearance.

Create a Multiple Items Form

1 Click the table or query from which you want to create the form.

2 Click the Create tab.

3 Click More Forms.

4 Click Multiple Items.

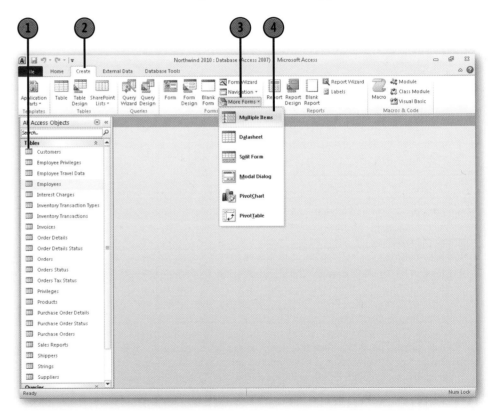

Modifying an Existing Form

Just as you can create a form from scratch, you can also open a form in Design view to add or delete controls, change a form's appearance, or add and delete fields. Form controls, such as check boxes, text boxes, and labels, enable you to provide

instructions for your colleagues and allow them to enter data as efficiently as possible. For example, if a field has two possible choices, such as true and false, you can create a check box that reflects those values by being either checked or unchecked.

Open a Form for Editing in Design View

① Display the forms in your database in the Navigation Pane.

② Right-click a form.

③ Click Design View.

See Also

For more information about modifying forms, see "Beautifying Forms and Reports" on page 145.

Display the Field List

1. Display a form in Design view.
2. Click the Design contextual tab.
3. If necessary, click Add Existing Fields.

Hide the Field List

- While the Field List task pane is displayed, click the Add Existing Fields button to hide it.

Add a Field to a Form

1. Drag the field from the Field List task pane to the desired spot on the form.

Tip

To display fields from other tables, display the Field List task pane and then click the Show All Tables link.

Adding and Deleting Form Controls

After you open a form in Design view, you can add or remove text boxes, option buttons, and images to and from the form. You can also modify a control's properties to change the control's appearance or to define where the control gets its data. Deleting unnecessary fields makes more room for the remaining fields and helps to control unwanted data entry. For example, if you find that your tables contain a field that some of your co-workers aren't supposed to fill in, such as a customer's credit limit, you can create a form that includes every table field and then delete the credit limit field.

Add a Control Using a Wizard

1 Open a form in Design view.

2 If necessary, click the Design contextual tab.

3 Click the Controls gallery's More button.

4 If the Use Control Wizards button is not highlighted, click it.

5 In the Controls gallery, click the control you want to add.

6 Drag the mouse pointer on the form to define the control's area.

7 Follow the steps in the wizard (if applicable) to define the contents of the control.

Delete a Control

1. Display a form in Design view.
2. Right-click the control.
3. Choose Delete from the shortcut menu.

Tip

Be sure to click the control itself, not a label next to the control.

Modify Control Properties

1. Display a form in Design view.
2. Click the control.
3. Click the Design contextual tab.
4. Click Property Sheet.
5. Click the property to change.
6. Follow any of these steps:
   - Type a new value in the text box next to the property name.
   - Click the down arrow and select a new value from the list that appears.
   - Click the Build button and use the dialog box that appears to select or construct a new value.

Available Control Types

Control	Description
Label	Text that is not tied to a field or other control.
Text box	A control that holds the contents of an existing table or query field or that has been typed by a user.
Toggle button	A button that can either be on or off, representing an independent value of on/off, true/false, or yes/no.
Option button	An independent option that represents an independent value. When grouped, only one option button may be selected at a time.
Check box	An independent option that can be selected or cleared. When two or more check boxes are included in the same Option Group control (mentioned elsewhere in this table), only one check box can be selected.
List box	A control that allows a user to pick a value from a list entered by the form's creator or that is derived from a table or query.
Combo box	A control that allows a user to enter a value or pick a value from a list entered by the form's creator or that is derived from a table or query.
Command button	A button that, when clicked, executes a macro or other set of instructions linked to the button.
Image	A control that holds an image or graphic.
Hyperlink	A control that provides a link to another object in the database, to a file on another computer, or to an Internet resource such as a Web page.

Control	Description
Chart	A control that summarizes data visually using a chart or graph.
Navigation control	A control that enables users to display, group, and interact with database objects without having to go through the Navigation Pane.
Unbound object frame	A control that holds a linked file.
Bound object frame	A control that holds an embedded file.
Page break	A control that separates a form into two (or more) printed pages.
Tab page	A control with multiple pages, accessed by folder tabs at the top of the control.
Attachment	A control that lets you attach a file to a form.
Subform/ Subreport	A form or report that displays records from a form or report on the "many" side of a one-to-many relationship.
Line	A control that lets you draw a line on a form.
Rectangle	A control that lets you draw a rectangle.
Option Group	An outline you place around a group of controls such as check boxes or option buttons. Only one control in the group can be selected at a time.
Web Browser control	A control that lets you display information from a Web site in an Access form.

Adding a Date Picker Control

It seems like using dates in Access, and in every other program for that matter, should be simple, but that's not always the case. Many Web applications, such as flight reservation systems, require you to enter dates using a date picker control that displays a month at a time. You can scroll from month to month and make your choice by clicking the day you want to leave when you display the right month.

You can add a similar control to your Access forms by creating a date picker control. This control, which is based on the date picker controls found in Microsoft Outlook 2010, enables users to decide on the date they want without you having to worry about whether 2/12/2010 means February 12, 2010 (as in the United States) or December 2, 2010 (as in many European countries).

Add a Date Picker

1. Open a form in Design view.
2. Click a form control that is bound to a field that contains dates.
3. If necessary, click the Design contextual tab.
4. If necessary, click Property Sheet.
5. Click Format.
6. Click Show Date Picker.
7. Click the down arrow that appears.
8. Click For Dates.

Tip

If you don't want Access to display a date picker for the selected field, set the Show Date Picker property's value to Never.

Creating a Subform

When you create a form that shows the records from a table on the "one" side of a one-to-many relationship, you can create a subform to display records from the table on the "many" side of the relationship. You can also change how the subform displays its records. If you want to see the records as a datasheet, you can change the subform's view so that it displays the related records while making best use of the form's space.

Add a Subform

1 Open a form based on a table on the "one" side of a one-to-many relationship in Design view.

2 Click the Design contextual tab.

3 Click the Controls gallery's More button.

4 Click the Subform/Subreport control.

5 On the form, drag to define the area where the subform should appear.

6 Select the Use An Existing Form option.

7 Click the form to supply the data for the subform.

8 Click Next.

9 Click Next to have the wizard draw the values from the form you selected.

10 Type Subform after the end of the form name.

11 Click Finish.

See Also

For more information about relationships, see "Creating Relationships between Tables" on page 44.

Tip ✓

You can get help with using subforms and subreports by going to the last page of the Subform Wizard and selecting the Display Help On Using Subforms or Subreports check box and clicking Finish.

Change Subform Views

1. Display the form that contains the subform in Form view.

2. Right-click any spot on the body of the subform.

3. Click Subform.

4. Click the desired view from the short-cut menu.

Tip

To change the subform from Datasheet view back to Form view, click the Design View button and then click the Form View button.

Displaying a Form and Its Datasheet Simultaneously.

Subforms enable you to display the data from two related tables or queries in a single form. What they don't enable you to do, however, is display the entire datasheet from which the form draws its data. If you create a subform that displays the same data as the main form, it displays only the current record, not the entire datasheet.

Create a Split Form

① Click the table to serve as the source of your form data.

② Click the Create tab.

③ Click More Forms.

④ Click Split Form.

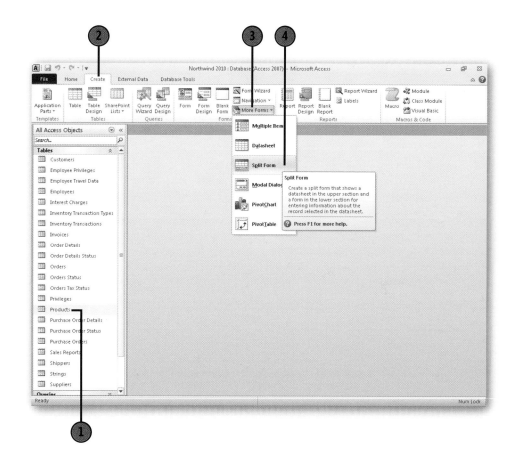

8 Creating Queries

Database tables store data, but even the best-designed table has limitations. For example, if a table holds more than a few dozen records, it's difficult to look through the table and find records that meet a particular criterion. You might, for example, want to display all orders from a specific customer without having to wade through the entire table to find them.

Enter the query. A query is a Microsoft Access 2010 object that lets you find just those table records you're interested in, whether you want to see all orders from customers in Germany or to identify customers who have never placed an order. You can also create queries that let you and your colleagues type the value for which they want to search. For example, rather than always search for orders by customers in Germany, you could create a query that asks which country to look for.

Introducing Query Types

When you want to retrieve table records that meet particular criteria, you create a query. The type of query you create, however, depends on the records you want to return and what, if anything, you want Access to do with the results.

The most basic query type is the select query, which reaches into one or more database tables and locates records. While you can have Access return every field in a record, you can also choose which fields are displayed in the results. For example, you could get information about customers that placed an order in a given month and, instead of displaying every field relating to the company, display just the company's name. You can also limit the records returned by the query by specifying one or more criteria or rules the query uses when

deciding which table rows to return. If your table contains data that relates to two different values, such as a company name and sales representatives, you can create a crosstab query to display the quantity of items sold by each employee to each company (as shown in the following figure).

A version of the select query is the parameter query. Like a select query, the parameter query uses one or more criteria to limit the records returned by the query. The difference, however, is that a parameter query lets the person running the query specify the criteria Access uses to decide whether or not to return a specific record. You can add a message to the criteria entry dialog box that lets the searcher know what kind of value to enter.

A separate type of query is the action query, which makes changes to the physical makeup of your database. You see two types of action queries in this chapter: the update query, which lets you change values in a table; and the make-table query, which writes query results to a new table in the current database (or another database entirely).

The final query type discussed in this section is the crosstab query. Unlike a select query, which presents its results in a worksheet, a crosstab query presents its results in a layout like that of a spreadsheet. Every value in the body of the query's results is related to two other values. In this case, those values are your suppliers and your product categories.

As in a spreadsheet, you can choose the mathematical operation Access uses to summarize the data in the body of the crosstab query's results. Available operations include finding a sum, average, the number of occurrences (as in the crosstab query results shown previously), or even the minimum or maximum value.

After you create a query (as shown following), you can display its results by double-clicking the query in the Navigation Pane. If the query is open in Design view, you can run it by clicking the Run button on the Design tab.

Creating a Query Using the Query Wizard

When you create a basic select query, you identify the table (or tables) with the data you want to find, name the fields to appear in the query results, and then save the query. The Query Wizard walks you through the process, making it easy to identify the tables and fields to appear in your query. What's more, you can choose whether to have Access display detailed results (that is, the individual query rows) or summarize the query's contents.

Create a Detail Query

1. Click the Create tab.

2. Click Query Wizard.

3. Click Simple Query Wizard.

4. Click OK.

Tip

To add all of a table's fields to your query, click the Add All (>>) button. You can also remove a field by clicking the Remove (<) button or remove all fields by clicking the Remove All (<<) button.

⑤ Click the Tables/Queries down arrow, and then click the table or query with the fields you want to use in your query.

⑥ Click the first field to include in the query's results.

⑦ Click Add.

⑧ Repeat steps 6 and 7 to add more fields (and step 5 to change the table or query from which you draw fields).

⑨ Click Next.

⑩ Click the Detail option button.

⑪ Click Next.

⑫ Type a name for your query.

⑬ Click Finish.

Tip

The step of the wizard that asks whether you want to create a detail or summary query appears only for some types of queries; don't panic if you don't see it.

Create a Summary Query

① Click the Create tab.

② Click Query Wizard.

③ Click Simple Query Wizard.

④ Click OK.

⑤ Click the Tables/Queries down arrow, and then click the table or query with the fields you want to use in your query.

⑥ Click the first field to include in the query's results.

⑦ Click Add.

⑧ Repeat steps 6 and 7 to add more fields (and step 5 to change the table or query from which you draw fields).

⑨ Click Next.

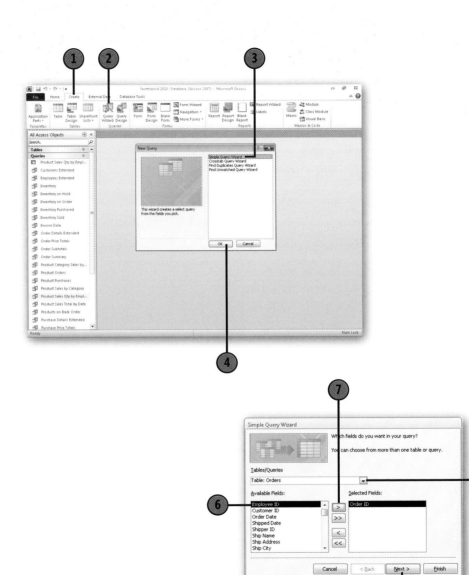

10 Click the Summary option button.

11 Click Summary Options.

12 Select the check boxes representing the summary values you want calculated.

13 Click OK.

14 Click Next.

15 Select the option button representing how you want the query to group rows in the query's source table.

16 Click Next.

17 Type a name for your query.

18 Click Finish.

Editing a Query in Design View

After you create a query, you can modify it by opening it in Design view. In Design view, you can add a table to the Query design area, add or remove query fields, or even add every field from a table in one step.

Open a Query for Editing

1. Display the queries in your database.
2. Right-click a query.
3. Click Design View.

Add a Table to a Query

1. Open the query in Design view.
2. Click the Show Table button.
3. Click the table to add.
4. Click Add.
5. Click Close.

Add a Field to a Query

1. Open the query in Design view.
2. Drag a field to a Field cell.

Tip

To add every field from a table to a query's results, drag the asterisk from the table's box in the table area to a Field cell in the Query design grid.

Tip

To enable a query with more than one table to return meaningful results, the two tables must be linked by a relationship.

Create a Query in Design View

1. Click the Create tab.
2. Click Query Design.
3. Click the first table or query you want to add.
4. Click Add.
5. Repeat steps 3 and 4 to add all the desired tables.
6. Click Close.
7. Drag fields to the design grid.
8. Click the Save button.
9. Type a name for the query.
10. Click OK.

Tip

To remove a table from the design grid, right-click the table's title bar and then click Remove Table.

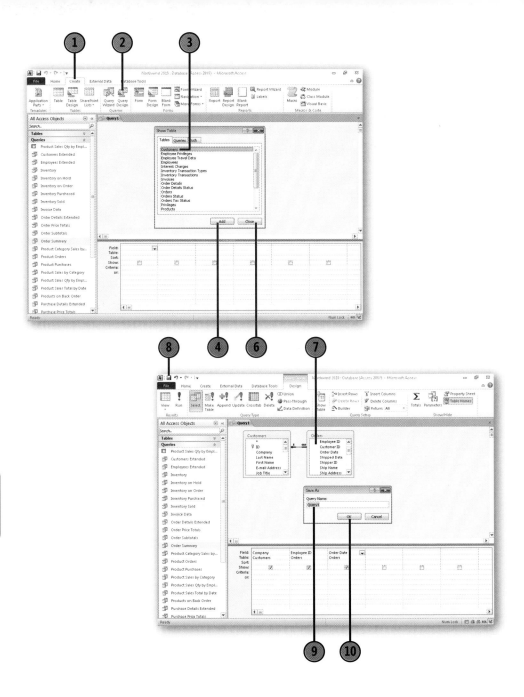

Using Criteria to Focus Query Results

It's unlikely that you'll want your query to find every record in a table—if you did, you could just open the table and not bother with the query! To limit the records a query locates, such as finding customers only in Germany, you can add criteria to the fields in the Query design grid.

Set Query Criteria

(1) Open a query in Design view.

(2) Click the Criteria cell for the field to which the criterion will be applied.

(3) Click Builder.

(4) Create the criterion in the Expression Builder.

(5) Click OK.

Tip

You can also type the criterion into the Criteria cell directly.

Tip

To use a text string, enclose the string in quotation marks (for example, "Germany"). If you forget, Access adds the quotes if it recognizes the criterion as a text string.

Introducing Operators

There are several types of database objects and tools you need to use when you create a criterion to narrow the records returned by a query or to calculate a value. The first set of objects to which you need to refer includes database tables and their fields. For example, to calculate the subtotal of a line in the Northwind sample database's Order Details table, multiply the Unit Price by the Quantity ordered, and adjust the total if the customer gets a discount (as noted in the Discount field). The expression to perform the first part of that calculation is [Order Details]![UnitPrice]*[Order Details]![Quantity].

Note that table fields are called out with the name of the table enclosed in square brackets, an exclamation point, and then the name of the field in square brackets.

Arithmetic Operators

Operator	Description
-	Subtraction (6-4=2)
*	Multiplication (6*4=24)
/	Division (6/4=1.5)
\	Integer division (6\4=1)
+	Addition (6+4=10)
Mod	Modular division (6 Mod 4=2)

Comparison Operators

Operator	Description
<	Less than
<=	Less than or equal to
<>	Not equal to
=	Equal to
>=	Greater than or equal to
>	Greater than
Between "Value1" And "Value2"	Between two values, inclusive (for example, Between "1" And "3" would return "1, 2, 3")

Logical Operators

Operator	Description
AND	Both elements of an expression must be true.
NOT	The expression must evaluate as false.
OR	At least one element of an expression must be true.
XOR	Exactly one element of an expression must be true, not both.

Using Queries to Calculate Values

One popular use for database tables is to maintain sales records with fields for the order identifier, the product ordered, and the product's price. What you can't do in a table is perform a calculation—the fields are just designed to hold data.

In a query, however, you can find totals, averages, or even the minimum or maximum value in the records found by your query.

Calculate a Value in a Query

1. Open a query in Design view.

2. Click Totals to add the Total row to the Query design grid.

3. Click the Field cell in the column in which you want to calculate the value.

4. Click Builder.

5. Build the calculation in the Expression Builder.

6. Click OK.

7. In the Field cell with the calculation, edit the value to the left of the colon to reflect the name you want for the field when the query results are displayed as a worksheet.

8. Click Run.

Tip

To select fields from other tables for use in a calculation, double-click the Tables icon in the left pane of the Expression Builder, double-click the table with the target field, and then double-click the field name in the center pane.

Creating a Parameter Query

Some of the time, you can create a query that always looks for the same information, such as orders from a specific country or the total orders from an established customer. Other times, however, you and your colleagues need the flexibility to enter a criterion (such as a country) into the query to focus the results correctly. You can do that by creating a parameter query, which lets you specify the criterion the query uses to find records.

Build a Parameter Query

① Open a query in Design view.

② Type the prompt surrounded by square brackets in the Criteria cell in the column representing the field in which you want to find the entered value.

③ Click Run to test the query.

④ Type a value in the message box that appears.

⑤ Click OK.

> **Caution!**
>
> If you don't type a prompt between the square brackets, the only indication you get to enter a parameter is a blank dialog box. If someone unfamiliar with the database runs the query, he or she will have no idea what to type in the box.

Finding Duplicate Records

The standard select query locates records that meet a criterion, such as orders made by a particular customer during a given month. However, you might also be interested in finding those customers who placed more than one order in a month. If all orders for a month are recorded in the same table, you could create a Find Duplicates query to locate CustomerID values that occur more than once in the table.

Create a Find Duplicates Query

1. Click the Create tab.
2. Click Query Wizard.
3. Click Find Duplicates Query Wizard.
4. Click OK.

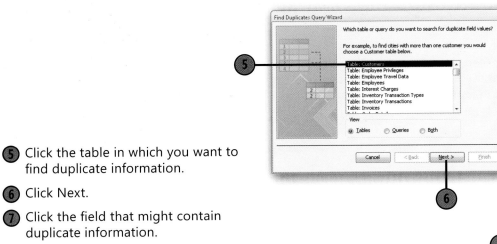

5 Click the table in which you want to find duplicate information.

6 Click Next.

7 Click the field that might contain duplicate information.

8 Click Add.

9 Repeat steps 7 and 8 to add any other fields to the query.

10 Click Next.

11 Click any other field you want to display in the query results.

12 Click Add.

13 Repeat steps 11 and 12 as necessary.

14 Click Next.

15 Type a name for the query.

16 Click Finish.

Finding Unmatched Records

When two tables are in a one-to-many relationship, you can create a Find Unmatched Records query to identify any records in the table on the "one" side that have no corresponding records in the table on the "many" side. For example, in the Northwind sample database, because the Customers and Orders tables are in a one-to-many relationship, you could identify customers that have never placed an order.

Create a Find Unmatched Records Query

1. Click the Create tab.
2. Click Query Wizard.
3. Click Find Unmatched Query Wizard.
4. Click OK.

Try This!

Open the Northwind sample database, click the Create tab, click the Query Wizard button, click Find Unmatched Query Wizard, and then click OK. Click Table: Customers and then click Next. In the next screen, click Table: Orders and then click Next. Verify that ID is highlighted in the Customers table and that CustomerID is highlighted in the Orders table; then click Next. Click Company, click the Add button, and then click Next. In the final screen, click Finish to accept the query name Access suggests. The query you create displays customers that have not placed an order.

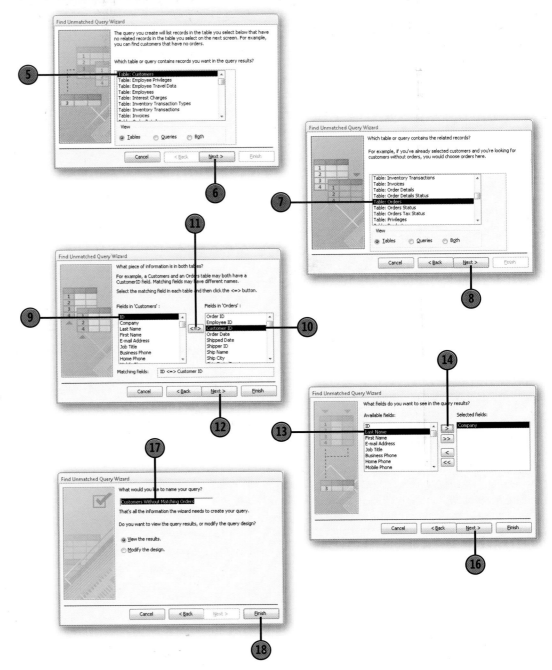

5 Click the table in which you want to find unmatched records.

6 Click Next.

7 Click the table or query with related records.

8 Click Next.

9 If necessary, click the field in the left pane that is in the table on the "one" side of the relationship.

10 If necessary, click the field in the right pane that is in the table on the "many" side of the relationship.

11 Click the Match button to identify the equivalent fields.

12 Click Next.

13 Click the name of a field to display in the query results.

14 Click Add.

15 Repeat steps 13 and 14 as needed to add fields to the display.

16 Click Next.

17 Type a name for the query.

18 Click Finish.

Writing Query Results to a New Table

When you run a query, Access writes the records the query finds into a dynaset, or dynamic record set. While Access remembers the results of queries you run, the results aren't actually written to a table, limiting what you can do with the data. You can, however, modify a select query so the results are written to a new table.

Create a Make-Table Query

1. Open a query in Design view.

2. Click Make Table.

3. Type a name for the new table.

4. Click OK.

5. Click Run.

6. Click Yes to create a new table that contains the selected records.

Tip

You can write the results of your query to a table in another database by selecting the Another Database option in the Make Table dialog box, clicking the Browse button, and using the file navigation dialog box to identify the database to receive the table.

Creating an Update Query

One exciting aspect of business is how quickly things change—of course, it can be difficult to keep track of all those changes! One useful task you can perform with an update query is to modify values in a table to reflect changes in your business environment. For example, if a supplier increases prices by 5 percent, you can create an update query that moves through your Products table and updates the records for that supplier's products.

Update Table Values with a Query

1. Open a query in Design view.

2. Click Update.

3. In the Criteria cell of the column you'll use to select the records to update, type the expression used to select which values should be updated.

4. In the Update To cell of the column that contains the value to be updated, type the expression used to update the values.

5. Click Run.

See Also

For more information about ensuring that table data is updated to reflect changes in a related table, see "Enforcing Referential Integrity" on page 46.

Creating a Crosstab Query

The basic means of storing and presenting data in Access is the table, which is essentially a list of information about a group of "things" (such as customer orders) related to a single primary key value. Another way to present data is in a crosstab query, which relates one value (such as a total or an average) with two other values (such as a customer and a month).

Build a Crosstab Query

1. Click the Create tab.
2. Click Query Wizard.
3. Click Crosstab Query Wizard.
4. Click OK.

5 Click the table or query to provide the values for your crosstab query.

6 Click Next.

7 Click the field to provide values for the row headings.

8 Click Add.

9 Click Next.

10 Click the field to provide values for the column headings.

11 Click Next.

12 Click the field to provide values for the data area (body) of the crosstab query.

13 Click the summary calculation to be performed on the values in the data area.

14 Click Next.

15 Type a name for the query.

16 Click Finish.

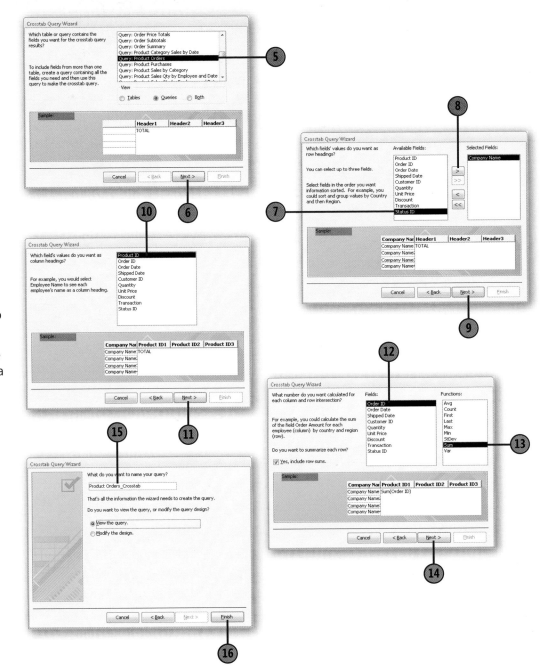

Finding the Largest and Smallest Values in a Field by Using a Query

When you create a query, you can have Access display a set number of the highest and lowest values in the query's results. You can also have Access display rows that contain the top or bottom values by asking Access to display a certain percentage of rows in the query's results. For example, if you reward the top 10 percent of your sales staff, you can create a query that sorts the query results according to the values in the

Total Sales field and displays the best values. When you filter a query's results by a percentage, you don't need to know the exact number of records in your table. In other words, if your sales staff is made up of 40 employees, creating a query that displays the top 10 percent of sales totals will return the top 4 representatives.

Find the Largest Values in a Field

1. Open a query in Design view.

2. Click the Sort cell of the field in which you want to find the top values.

3. Click the down arrow that appears.

4. Click Descending.

5. If necessary, click the Design tab.

6. Using the Top Values field control, perform any of these tasks:

   • Click the control's down arrow and select a default value to specify the number of values or the percentage of values to display.

   • Type a number indicating the number of values you want displayed in the query results.

   • Type a percentage indicating the portion of the table's rows you want displayed in the query results.

7. Click Run.

Find the Smallest Values in a Field

① Open a query in Design view.

② Click the Sort cell of the field in which you want to find the top values.

③ Click the down arrow that appears.

④ Click Ascending.

⑤ If necessary, click the Design tab.

⑥ Using the Top Values field control, perform any of these tasks:

- Click the control's down arrow and select a default value to specify the number of values or the percentage of values to display.

- Type a number indicating the number of values you want displayed in the query results.

- Type a percentage indicating the portion of the table's rows you want displayed in the query results.

⑦ Click Run.

Tip

To have your query display all its results, return to Design view, click the Design tab, click the Top Values field's down arrow, and then click All.

Creating Reports

Reports give you the ability to present your table and query data in an accessible format. In some ways, reports and forms are very similar—both types of database objects let you display your table records and query results at one record per page, in a series of columns or rows, or in a custom layout you create in Design view. The difference between forms and reports is that in addition to presenting your table and query data, reports let you summarize your data. For example, you can create a report that not only lists every order made by every customer but also finds the total amount of all orders for a particular customer. It's possible to do the same thing with queries, but the Report Wizard streamlines the process greatly, saving you time and effort while producing valuable information.

Creating a Report Using the Report Wizard

Although it might be possible to generate useful reports from the data in a single table or query, it's very likely that you'll want to combine data from more than one table or query into a single report. For example, you might have product data in one table and supplier data in another table and then want to create a report in which full supplier contact information accompanies the product information. You can do that by creating a report using the Report Wizard.

Step through the Report Wizard

1 Click the Create tab.

2 Click Report Wizard.

3 Click the down arrow and then choose the first table or query from which you want to draw values for the report.

4 Click a field in the Available Fields box and then click either of the following buttons:

- Add to add the selected field.

- Add All to add all fields to the report.

5 Click Next.

- If you created a report based on a query that reads in primary key values from more than one table, a wizard page appears asking you to select preliminary grouping criteria for the report's records. Click the name of the field by which you want to group and then click Next.

6 If necessary, click the first field by which you want to group the report's contents and then click Add. Repeat to add grouping levels.

7 Click Next.

8 Click the first field's down arrow and click the first field by which you want to sort the report's contents.

9 If necessary, click the Sort Options button to toggle between Ascending or Descending.

10 Click Next.

11 Use the controls on the remaining wizard pages to select a layout, page orientation, style, and name for the report. When you're done, click Finish.

Tip

You can remove fields from the Selected Fields pane of the Report Wizard by clicking the field name and then clicking either Remove (to remove the selected field) or Remove All (to remove all fields).

See Also

For information about changing report grouping levels, see "Grouping Report Records" on page 139.

Creating a Summary Report

Although both database object types let you display your table and query records, one thing you can do in a report that you can't with a form is to summarize your data within a report. For example, if you created a summary report of all orders and grouped the report's contents by product, you could add a summary function to find the total sales for each product. You could also find the minimum, maximum, or average value of orders for each listed product.

Build a Summary Report

① Click the Create tab.

② Click Report Wizard.

③ Click the down arrow and then choose the first table or query from which you want to draw values for the report.

④ Click a field in the Available Fields box and then click either of the following buttons:

- Add to add the selected field.

- Add All to add all fields to the report.

⑤ Click Next.

- If you created a report based on a query that reads in primary key values from more than one table, a wizard page appears asking you to select preliminary grouping criteria for the report's records. Click the name of the field by which you want to group and then click Next.

⑥ Click the first field by which you want to group the report's contents and then click Add. Repeat to add grouping levels.

⑦ Click Next.

⑧ Click the first field's down arrow and click the first field by which you want to sort the report's contents.

⑨ Click the sort options button to toggle between Ascending or Descending.

⑩ Click Summary Options.

⑪ Select the check box representing the target field and summary operation.

⑫ Select the option indicating whether to display the summary alone or details (report rows) and the summary.

⑬ Click OK.

⑭ Click Next.

⑮ Use the controls on the remaining wizard pages to select a layout, page orientation, style, and name for the report. Click Finish when you're done.

Tip

You can select more than one field and summary function—every summary you choose will appear in your finished report.

Creating a Report in Design View

The Report Wizard makes it easy to create reports, but you can also create a blank form in Design view and start adding controls on your own. If the report will consist only of a few fields, and you want to place the fields in particular locations, you might want to create the report in Design view, rather than creating it using a wizard and then editing the result in Design view. Of course, you might just prefer working in Design view!

Build a New Report

1. Click the Create tab.

2. Click Report Design.

3. If necessary, on the Design contextual tab, click Add Existing Fields.

4. If necessary, in the Field List task pane, click Show All Tables.

5. In the Field List task pane, click the show detail control next to the table to provide fields or the report.

6. Drag fields from the Field List task pane to the report's Detail section.

7. Click Save.

8. Type a name for the report.

9. Click OK.

Try This!

In the Northwind sample database, click the Create tab and then click Report Design. Click Add Existing Fields, click Show All Tables, and click the show detail control next to the Products table. Drag the Product Name, Description, and List Price fields to the form's Detail section. Click Save, type a name for the report, and then click OK.

Modifying an Existing Report

Once you create a report, you can open it in Design view and add or remove fields. The available fields appear in the Field List task pane; to add a field, just drag its name from the Field List task pane to the body of the report.

See Also

For more information about modifying reports, see "Beautifying Forms and Reports" on page 145.

Open a Report for Editing

1. Display the database's reports in the Navigation Pane.

2. Right-click a report.

3. Click Design View.

Tip

When you have a report open in Design view, you can also display the Field List task pane by pressing Alt+F8.

Display or Hide the Field List Task Pane

- Click Add Existing Fields to display or hide the Field Task pane.

Add a Field to a Report

① Drag the field from the Field List task pane to the desired spot on the form.

Adding and Deleting Report Controls

After you create a report, you can add controls like labels, text boxes, check boxes, and option buttons to display your table and query data. The specific steps you take to add a control and define its data source depend on the control you want to create, but the control wizards are there to help you through the process.

When you create a control, you actually create a control (such as a text box) and a label identifying the control. You can delete, modify, or move the label without affecting its associated control.

Add a Control Using a Wizard

1. Open a report in Design view.

2. If necessary, click the Design tab.

3. If necessary, click the Controls gallery's More button.

4. Click Use Control Wizards.

5. Click the control you want to add.

6. Drag the mouse pointer on the report to define the control's area.

7. If a control wizard appears, follow its steps to define the contents of the control. If not, you can modify the control using the formatting techniques found in this section and in Section 10, "Beautifying Forms and Reports."

Delete a Control

1 Right-click the control you want to delete.

2 Click Delete.

See Also

For more information about controls and control types, see the table "Available Control Types" on page 97.

Modify Control Properties

1 Open the report in Design view.

2 Click the control.

3 Click Property Sheet.

4 Click the property to change.

5 Follow one of these steps:

- Type a new value in the text box next to the property name.

- Click the down arrow, and select a new property from the list that appears.

- Click the Build button and use the dialog box that appears to select or construct a new value.

Tip

When you delete a control, be sure to click the control itself—not the label next to the control.

Tip

You can change the value in a control's label by editing the label directly or by setting the control's Caption property.

Calculating Values in a Report

When you create a report, you can create a control (such as a text box) that performs a calculation on the values elsewhere in the report. For example, if a report record had a field for a product's Price and another field noting the Quantity ordered, you can create a control that multiplies the values from those fields and displays the result. Creating calculated fields in a report is handy when you work with a popular query and you don't want Microsoft Access 2010 to recalculate the values every time the query is run.

Create a Calculated Field

1. Open a report in Design view.

2. If necessary, click the Design tab.

3. Click the Text Box control.

4. In the report Detail section, drag to define the area for the text box.

5. If necessary, click the Property Sheet button to display the control's properties.

6. If necessary, click the Data tab.

7. In the Control Source field, type = followed by the expression used to calculate the field's value and then press Tab.

8. Type a new value for the text box's label.

See Also

For information about calculating summary values in a report, as opposed to calculating a value based on the current record, see "Creating a Summary Report" on page 130.

Tip

Clicking the Build button to the right of the Control Source property opens the Expression Builder.

Introducing Report Sections

A basic report has five sections:

- Report Header
- Page Header
- Detail
- Page Footer
- Report Footer

The Report Header section holds information that appears at the top of the first page of the printed report. Typical information you find in the Report Header includes the title of the report, the logo of the company producing the report, and the report's author.

The Page Header, by contrast, contains information that appears at the top of every printed report page. Most frequently, you find the report's column headings, page numbers, and dates in this report area, but you can also put smaller versions of a company logo in this area to identify the report's origins. If the report data is confidential, this area (and the Report Header) is a good place to note that, as the annotation appears on every page.

The Page Footer and Report Footer sections are the complement of the Page Header and Report Header sections. Information in the Page Footer section appears at the bottom of every printed report page, while information in the Report Footer section appears at the bottom of the last printed report page.

The report's Detail section is where the table records or query results appear. Whether the Detail section has one or more than one record depends on how you set up your report. As with any report section, you can add other controls, text, or drawing objects to make your data easier to comprehend.

If you add a grouping level to a report, Access 2010 lets you add a header and footer section named after the field used to group the report's contents. For example, if you group the contents of a report based on a query combining data from the Customers, Orders, and Order Details tables, you could group the report's contents by the country of the customer. If you did, two sections named Country Header and Country Footer would appear in the report, flanking the Detail section.

Grouping Report Records

When you create a report using the Report Wizard, you can define how the report's records are grouped. For example, you can create a report based on the Northwind sample database's Orders and Order Details tables and group records by Customer ID. If you want to display each customer's orders by the date they were placed, you can create a second grouping level based on the Order Date field.

When you add a grouping level to a report, Access 2010 adds a header corresponding to the grouping field's name. If you group a set of products by their category name, Access 2010 creates a CategoryName Header; if you like, you can add a CategoryName Footer as well.

Create a Grouping Level

1. Open a report in Layout view.

2. Click the Design tab.

3. In the Grouping & Totals group, click Group & Sort.

4. Click Add A Group.

5. Click the field by which you want to group the report's contents.

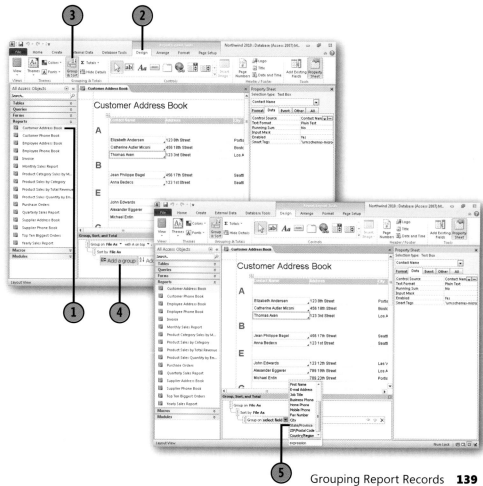

Reorder Grouping Levels

1. Open a grouped report in Layout view.

2. Click the Design tab.

3. If necessary, click Group & Sort.

4. Click the grouping level you want to move.

5. Follow either of these steps:

   • Click the Move Up button to move the grouping level higher in the order.

   • Click the Move Down button to move the grouping level down in the order.

Delete a Grouping Level

1. Open a grouped report in Layout view.

2. Click the Design tab.

3. If necessary, click Group & Sort.

4. Click the grouping level you want to delete.

5. Click the Delete button.

Creating a Subform or Subreport

An Access 2010 database often has a number of relationships between tables. In the Northwind sample database, for example, Suppliers make Products, which are part of Orders placed by Customers. When two tables are in a one-to-many relationship, you can create a report based on the contents of the table on the "one" side of the relationship and add a subreport displaying related records from the table on the "many" side of the relationship. The Customers and Orders tables are in a one-to-many relationship (they have the Customer ID field in common), so you could create a report listing every customer and add a subreport displaying all orders placed by the current customer.

Add a Subform or Subreport

1. Open a report in Design view.
2. Click the Design tab.
3. Click the Controls gallery's More button.
4. Click the Subform/Subreport control.
5. In the Detail section of the report, drag to define the area where the subform or subreport should appear.
6. Select the Use An Existing Report Or Form option.
7. Click the report or form to supply the data for the subform or subreport.
8. Click Next.
9. Click the relationship from which Access 2010 should create the subform or subreport.
10. Click Next.
11. As appropriate, type **Subform** or **Subreport** after the end of the suggested name.
12. Click Finish.

See Also

For more information about relationships, see "Creating Relationships between Tables" on page 44.

Creating Mailing Labels

One frequent use for contact information in a database is to create a set of mailing labels so you can send special offers or notes of appreciation to all or a subset of your customers or suppliers. The Label Wizard walks you through the process, letting you choose the type of label on which you print, pick the table and query fields you want printed on the labels, and add any punctuation or other text to each label.

Generate Mailing Labels

1. Click the database object from which you want to create your mailing labels.

2. Click the Create tab.

3. Click Labels.

4. Click the label size you want to print onto.

5. Click Next twice to select the label and accept the default font settings.

 See Also

For more information about how grouping and sorting affect the order of records on a report, see "Grouping Report Records" on page 139.

(6) Click the first field to appear on the label.

(7) Click Add.

(8) Click the position on the label for the next field.

- Repeat steps 6 to 8 to add all desired fields to the label.

(9) If desired, type any text (such as punctuation) you want to appear on the label.

(10) Click Next.

(11) Click the first field to use as the sort criteria for the labels.

(12) Click Add.

- Repeat steps 11 and 12 to add additional sort criteria.

(13) Click Next.

(14) Type a name for the report and click Finish.

Tip

You should always print one test page of mailing labels on regular paper to be sure everything lines up correctly and looks the way you want it to.

Tip

Line breaks aren't accepted in the Label Wizard. To position text on the label's next line, click the line.

10

Beautifying Forms and Reports

After you create forms and reports to display your table and query data, you can change the appearance of any control on the form or report. You can change the appearance of individual elements in your Microsoft Access 2010 objects, but an easier way to change the format of every object at once is to use an Office theme that is included with Access 2010. You can use an Office theme as it is out of the box, or you can create and modify your own Office themes so you can make the appearance of your forms and reports consistent.

Another useful Access 2010 capability is to create a conditional format, which changes the appearance of the data in a text box based on the data's value. If a customer hasn't placed an order in the last year, a product has been discontinued, or a shipment took more than a week to arrive, you can use conditional formats to highlight that data and bring it to your attention quickly.

Formatting Text

Access 2010 is a great program for storing your data efficiently, but it also gives you a lot of flexibility in choosing how to display data in forms and reports. One important part of designing a form or report is choosing formats for each element of the design: labels, headings, and data. Corporate logos, color schemes, and documents can help guide initial development, but you should always listen to your colleagues to discover ways to make the text on your forms and reports easier to understand. Opening a form or report in Design view lets you make your changes, but feel free to switch between Design view and either Form view or Print Preview (for reports) to see how your changes will look in the finished document.

Change Text Formatting

1. Select the text to be formatted.

2. Click the Home tab.

3. Use the Ribbon buttons in the Text Formatting group to format your text.

Tip

You can also view and change an object's appearance by clicking the object, clicking Property Sheet on the Design tab, clicking the Format tab, and setting the image's formatting properties.

Introducing Office Themes

Microsoft Office 2010 includes powerful design tools that enable you to create attractive, professional documents quickly. The Access 2010 product team implemented new design capabilities by allowing you to apply Office themes to your database objects. A *theme* is a way to specify the fonts, colors, and graphic effects that appear in a database. Access 2010 comes with many themes installed.

To apply an existing Office theme, open a form or report in Design view. Then, in the Design tab's Themes group, click Themes, and click the theme you want to apply to your database. By default, Access 2010 applies the Office theme to your database objects.

When you want to format a database element, Access 2010 displays a set of standard colors, which remains the same regardless of which theme is applied, and a set of colors that are available within the active theme. The theme colors appear in the top segment of the color palette; the standard colors and the More Colors link, which displays the Colors dialog box, appear at the bottom of the palette. If you format Access 2010 objects using colors from the theme colors portion of the color palette, applying a different theme changes that object's colors.

You can create your own themes by modifying an existing theme and then selecting the new fonts and colors to be applied to your database objects. After you've made your changes, you can save your theme so it will be available for all your Microsoft Office 2010 files, not just your Access 2010 database objects.

Applying Office Themes

Rather than define the format of every object in your forms and reports, you can apply one of the Office themes installed with Access 2010. Office themes let you do more than just apply an existing format, however; you can choose which elements of an Office theme to apply, create new Office themes to match the formatting of an existing form or report, or modify an existing Office theme.

Select an Office Theme

1. Open the form or report you want to format in Design view.
2. Click the Design tab.
3. Click Themes.
4. Click the Office theme you want to apply.

Caution

You can't permanently change a built-in Office theme; you can only change an Office theme you created.

Apply Office Theme Elements

1. Open the form or report you want to format in Design view.
2. Click the Design tab.
3. Click Colors and then click the color set you want to apply.
4. Click Fonts and then click the font you want to apply.

Combine Existing Elements into a New Office Theme

① Open the form or report you want to format in Design view.

② Click the Design tab.

③ Click Colors and then click the desired color set.

④ Click Fonts and then click the font you want to apply.

⑤ Click Themes.

⑥ Click Save Current Theme.

⑦ Type a name for the Office theme.

⑧ Click Save.

Caution

You can't permanently change a built-in Office theme; you can only change an Office theme you created.

Tip

To delete an Office theme, display a form or report in Design view, click Themes, and then click Save Current Theme. In the Save Current Theme dialog box, click the theme you want to delete and then press the Delete key.

Create a Custom Office Theme

1. Open a form or report in Design view.

2. Click the Design tab.

3. Click Colors.

4. Click Create New Theme Colors.

5. Select a new color for each theme element.

6. Type a name for the new color set.

7. Click Save.

8. Click Fonts.

9. Click Create New Theme Fonts.

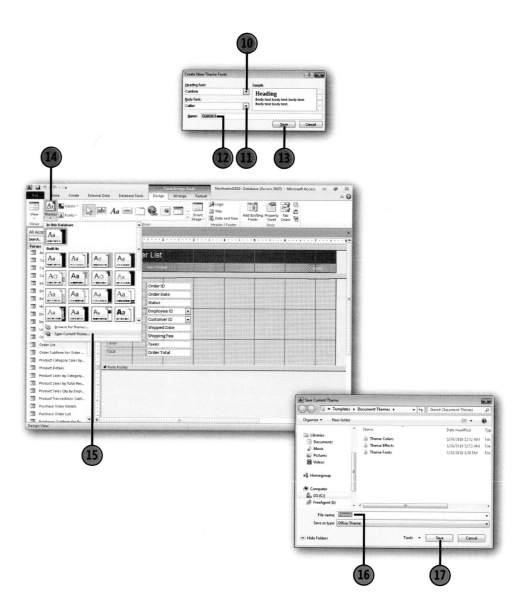

10 Select a new Heading font.

11 Select a new Body font.

12 Type a name for the new font set.

13 Click Save.

14 Click Themes.

15 Click Save Current Theme.

16 Type a name for the theme.

17 Click Save.

Setting Control Appearance

Once you add controls to a form or report, you can change the
appearance of those controls by displaying the Design tab and
using the buttons in the Font group. You can change the color
of any control element as well as being able to apply special
effects to the controls, changing how they're drawn on the
form or report. You can also use the commands on the Ribbon's Arrange tab to arrange and distribute your controls
attractively.

Change Control Colors

1. Right-click the control you want to format.

2. Follow either of these steps:

   - Click the Fill/Back Color menu item and choose a color
     for the control's background elements.

   - Click the Font/Fore Color menu item and choose a
     color for the control's foreground and text elements.

Tip

You can also change a control's appearance by clicking the
control, clicking Property Sheet, clicking the Format tab, and
changing the control's formatting properties.

Format Controls with Special Effects

1. Right-click the control you want to format.

2. Point to the Special Effect menu item.

3. Click the effect you want to apply to the control.

Caution

Applying the Etched and Chiseled special effects removes an object's fill and line/border color settings.

Tip

You can change the color of a shadow by changing the object's line color.

Distribute Controls Horizontally

1. Display the form or report in Design view.

2. Select the controls you want to distribute on the form or report.

3. If necessary, click the Arrange tab.

4. Click Size/Space and then follow any of these steps:

   - Click Equal Horizontal to space the selected controls evenly.

   - Click Increase Horizontal to push the selected controls farther apart.

   - Click Decrease Horizontal to pull the selected controls closer together.

Tip

It's usually a good idea to click Equal Horizontal first so your controls will be a uniform distance apart before you use the Increase Horizontal or Decrease Horizontal items to change your controls' layout.

Tip

You can select multiple controls by holding down the Ctrl key and clicking the controls, or by holding down the left mouse button and dragging to select the controls you want to reformat.

Distribute Controls Vertically

① Display the form or report in Design view.

② Select the controls you want to distribute on the form or report.

③ If necessary, click the Arrange tab.

④ Click Size/Space and then follow any of these steps:

- Click Equal Vertical to space the selected controls evenly.

- Click Increase Vertical to push the selected controls farther apart.

- Click Decrease Vertical to pull the selected controls closer together.

Try This!

Open the Northwind sample database, click Forms on the Shutter Bar, right-click Product Details, and then click Design View. Select the Product Code, Product Name, Description, and Category labels. On the Ribbon, click the Arrange tab, click the Size/Space button, and then click Decrease Vertical. The labels move closer together. To return the labels to their previous spacing, click the Size/Space button and then click Increase Vertical. Click the Close box to close the form.

Align Controls

1 Select the controls you want to align.

2 Click the Arrange tab.

3 Click Align and then follow any of these steps:

- Click Left to align the selected objects by their left edges.

- Click Right to align the selected objects by their right edges.

- Click Top to align the selected objects by their top edges.

- Click Bottom to align the selected objects by their bottom edges.

- Click To Grid to move each object to the nearest point on the design grid.

Tip ✓

If you want to help ensure that your objects are aligned, click the Arrange tab on the Ribbon. Then, in the Control Layout group, click the Size/Space button and click Snap to Grid. Turning on the grid limits where you can place your objects; if you want to place an object so it isn't aligned with the design grid, hold down the Ctrl key while you move the object.

Tip ✓

For even more control over your form and report controls' appearance, click the control you want to modify, click the Design tab on the Ribbon, click Property Sheet, click the Format tab, and set the properties using the tools in the Property Sheet task pane.

Adding Lines, Shapes, and Borders

When you create a control to display form and report data, you also create a label that you can modify to identify the data presented in the control. Although labels are a great help in identifying the source of your form and report data, they only go so far in identifying groups of controls. For example, if you were to create a report from the contents of a Products table, you could separate general information about a product (such as its category and supplier) from the more specific information by drawing a line between the two groups of controls.

Draw a Line

1. Open a form or report in Design view.

2. If necessary, click the Design tab.

3. Click the Controls gallery's More button.

4. Click the Line control.

5. In the body of the form or report, drag the mouse pointer to create the line.

Add a Border

1. Open a form or report in Design view.

2. Click the control to which you want to add a border.

3. If necessary, click the Format tab.

4. Click Shape Outline.

5. Click the color you want to apply to the border.

Tip

In Design view, objects have lines drawn around them to indicate their real size, so they might appear to have a border when they don't. If you're not sure, view the form in Form view or a report in Print Preview to see whether there is a border.

Change an Object's Fill Color

1. Open a form or report in Design view.

2. Select the object you want to format.

3. Click the Format tab.

4. Click Shape Fill.

5. Click the color you want to fill the object.

Showing Gridlines in a Report

Access 2010 facilitates form and report design by enabling you to "snap" your form and report controls to a grid. When the grid is turned on, Access 2010 limits where you can move your controls. Drawing lines through the allowable spots forms a grid of horizontal and vertical lines on your form or report's body. If you'd like to make those gridlines visible on your form or report, you can turn them on quickly. The gridlines are black by default, but you can change their color, line style, and thickness by using the controls in the Gridlines menu on the Arrange tab. Feel free to play around with different gridline appearances until you find the setting combination that looks the best on your form or report.

Turn Gridlines On or Off

1. Open a form or report in Design view.
2. Click the Arrange tab.
3. Click Size/Space.
4. Click the Grid menu item to alternate between showing and hiding gridlines.

Change Gridline Appearance

1 Open a form or report in Design view.

2 Click the Arrange tab.

3 Click any object on the form or report.

4 Click the Gridlines button and then follow any of these steps:

- Click one of the gridline options to select which gridlines to display.

- Click the Color button and then click the desired gridline color.

- Click the Width button and then click the desired gridline width option.

- Click the Border button and then click the desired gridline style option.

See Also

For more information on aligning report controls to the grid, see "Setting Control Appearance" on page 132.

Coloring Alternate Rows in a Form or Report

You can create forms and reports that display one table or query record per page, but viewing data one record at a time can take away your ability to relate one record to the next. Viewing multiple records on a form or report helps you spot patterns in your data, but distinguishing one row from another can be difficult unless you change the formatting to make the rows stand out from their neighbors. In Access 2010, you can format your form or report so that alternating data rows have a different background color. You can choose whichever color combinations you'd like, but bear in mind that a combination that works well on screen might not work well on the printed page. Test your choices to figure out which combinations best meet your needs.

Color Alternate Data Rows

1 Display a form in Datasheet view.

2 If necessary, click the Datasheet tab.

3 Click Alternate Row Color.

4 Click the color you want to apply to alternate worksheet form rows.

Adding a Totals Row to a Worksheet

Previous versions of Access enabled you to add summary calculations to your reports, but if you viewed your data as a worksheet, the worksheet itself didn't contain the summary. That meant you either had to create a report that contained a summary calculation at the end, build a query that totaled the values in one or more fields, or do some quick mental arithmetic. In Access 2010, you can add a Totals row to a worksheet, bypassing the need to create a specific report or query to calculate the total.

Add a Totals Row

1. Display a form in Datasheet view.

2. Click the Home tab.

3. In the Records group, click Totals.

4. In the new Total row, click the cell in the column you want to summarize.

5. Click the down arrow that appears.

6. Click the summary operation you want.

See Also

For more information on adding a summary calculation to a report, see "Calculating Values in a Report" on page 137.

Adding a Picture

The Chinese philosopher Confucius said that a picture is worth 10,000 words. His wisdom still holds true—a photograph of a product or a diagram of a process can provide valuable contextual information to help you and your colleagues understand form and report data. Also, whether you work for yourself or for a large organization, it's important to add your logo to any documents you want to distribute outside your organization.

Another important consideration when adding a picture to an Access 2010 object is whether to embed the picture in the file, which increases the database file's size every time you use the picture or to link to a single copy of the picture that travels everywhere with the database. If you use that image frequently or if it's a large file, you should choose to link to the file instead of embedding it.

Embed a Picture

1. Open a form or report in Design view.

2. If necessary, click the Design tab.

3. Click Insert Image.

4. Click Browse.

5. Browse for the picture you want to insert and double-click it.

6. Drag to define the size of the image.

Change an Embedded Picture to a Linked Picture

(1) Open the form or report containing the picture in Design view.

(2) Click the embedded picture.

(3) If necessary, click the Design tab.

(4) Click Property Sheet.

(5) If necessary, click the Format tab.

(6) Click the Picture Type box.

(7) Click the down arrow.

(8) Click Linked.

(9) In the dialog box that appears, click No to keep the current image in the image frame.

See Also

For more information about adding borders to your pictures, see "Adding Lines, Shapes, and Borders" on page 156.

Applying Conditional Formatting

Changing the appearance of your form and report data by applying formats (or AutoFormats) makes your data easier to read. However, you may want to apply different formats to a control's contents based on the data's value. For example, you might want to highlight the names of any customers who are within 10 percent of their credit limit or display information about discontinued products in red.

Define a Conditional Format

1. Open a form or report in Design view.

2. Click the control to which you want to apply a conditional format.

3. Click the Format tab.

4. Click Conditional Formatting.

5. Click New Rule.

6. Click the comparison phrase field's down arrow and then click the desired comparison.

7. Type values into the value fields to define the condition's parameters.

8. Use the Bold, Italic, Underline, Fill Color, Font Color, and Enabled buttons to define the conditional format.

9. Click OK.

10. If desired, repeat steps 5 through 9 to create another rule.

11. Click OK.

Tip

If you create multiple conditions, make sure there is no overlap between the conditions, such as one condition checking whether a number is less than 3,000 and another checking whether the same number is less than 1,500. If there is overlap, the first condition Access 2010 checks is applied. The proper way to create the conditions is to check in Condition 1 if a value is between 1,500 and 3,000, and then check in Condition 2 if the value is less than 1,500.

Caution

If you change the appearance of a control's contents by making the contents bold or increasing the font size, be sure the control is large enough to display the data.

Define a Data Bar Conditional Format

① Open a form or report in Design view.

② Click the control to which you want to apply a conditional format.

③ Click the Format tab.

④ Click Conditional Formatting.

⑤ Click New Rule.

⑥ Click Compare to Other Records.

⑦ Click the Bar Color control's down arrow and click a color for the data bar.

⑧ Click OK.

⑨ Click OK.

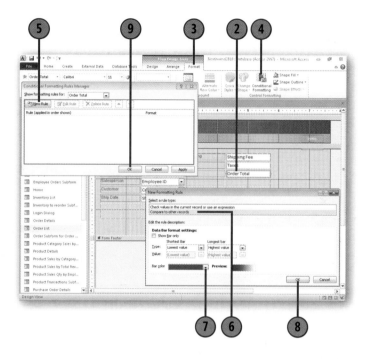

Changing the Source of an Image

If you work with one organization for a while, you'll probably need to change the images on some of your forms and reports. Whether the change is to update a product's photograph or to change from an old department logo to a new one, you can make the change quickly by identifying the new image in the control's Picture property. The advantage of making the change in the Property Sheet task pane is that you can save time by not deleting and replacing the previous image. Another consideration is that the image is placed in the same control, meaning you won't have to resize the image.

Define a New Image Source

1. Open the form that contains the image in Design view.

2. Click the image you want to change.

3. If necessary, click the Design tab.

4. Click Property Sheet.

5. Click the Format tab.

6. Click Picture.

7. Click the Build button.

8. Click the new target image file.

9. Click Open.

Setting Image Alignment and Backing Color

When you add an image to a form or report, you actually create a control and designate the image as the contents of that control. Because the image is contained within a control, you can use the edges of the control as a frame through which you view the image. As an example, suppose that you have a large image illustrating a process, but the two critical areas you need to show on a form are in opposite corners of the image.

align the image so any corner is displayed, meaning you can display the sections of the image you need to show without cropping, editing, or otherwise mangling the image itself. If there is space between the edge of the image and the control's border, you can fill the rest of the control with a background color to provide a frame around the image.

Set a Backing Color

1. Open the form that contains the image in Design view.

2. Click the image you want to change.

3. If necessary, click the Design tab.

4. Click Property Sheet.

5. Click the Format tab.

6. Click Back Color.

7. Click the Build button.

8. Click the desired color.

See Also

For more information about formatting the borders of a control, see "Adding Lines, Shapes, and Borders" on page 156.

Change a Picture's Alignment

1. Open the form that contains the image in Design view.

2. Click the image you want to change.

3. If necessary, click the Design tab.

4. Click Property Sheet.

5. Click the Format tab.

6. Click Picture Alignment.

7. Click the down arrow.

8. Click the desired alignment.

Tip

If you want to see the Detail section of the form or any objects behind the image, change the Back Style property's value to Transparent.

Tiling a Picture

When you add an image to a form or report, you usually want the image to appear in one place. Some images are meant to be repeated, however. For example, you could create a small, square graphic with a repeating pattern, or texture, that you'd like to appear as the background for your form or report. When you repeat an image, you use instances of the image like tiles in a mosaic—the images are placed side by side and cover the entire inside of your image control.

Repeat a Picture on a Form or Report

1 Open the form that contains the image in Design view.

2 Click the image you want to change.

3 If necessary, click the Design tab.

4 Click Property Sheet.

5 Click the Format tab.

6 Click Picture Tiling.

7 Click the down arrow.

8 Click Yes.

> **Tip**
>
> You can buy textures in most software stores or create your own with a graphics program. The keys to creating a great texture are to make sure you can't see the edges of the individual graphics and to keep the texture file as small as possible.

Setting Image Height and Width

When you design a form or report, you often have the freedom to move things around and make images as large or small as you need to create an attractive design. There are times, however, when space on the page is at a premium and you need to restrict the space an image takes up. You can set the height and width of an image control by setting its Height and Width properties in the Property Sheet task pane.

You can also change how an image will react when you resize its control. If you want, you can have the image stretch to match the new frame size, remain the same size (and possibly have part of the image be hidden), or resize the image to fit within the control while retaining the original height and width ratio.

Set a Precise Image Height and Width

1. Open the form that contains the image in Design view.

2. Click the image you want to change.

3. If necessary, click the Design tab.

4. Click Property Sheet.

5. Click the Format tab.

6. In the Width field, type the desired width.

7. In the Height field, type the desired height.

Tip

If you add an image to a form or report and want to ensure that all other images you add to other database objects are the same size as that image, write down the values in the Height and Width property boxes.

Set an Image's Resizing Property

(1) Open the form that contains the image in Design view.

(2) Click the image you want to change.

(3) If necessary, click the Design tab.

(4) Click Property Sheet.

(5) Click the Format tab.

(6) Click Size Mode.

(7) Click the down arrow.

(8) Click the desired size mode.

See Also

For information about changing how an image is aligned within a control, see "Setting Image Alignment and Backing Color" on page 167.

11

Creating Charts in Access 2010

When you enter data into a Microsoft Access 2010 database table, you create a record of important events, whether they are individual product sales, sales for an hour of a day, or product prices. What a long list of table values in cells can't communicate easily, however, are the overall trends in the data. The best way to communicate trends in a large collection of data is by creating a chart that summarizes data visually.

You have a great deal of control over your chart's appearance—you can change the color of any chart element, modify a chart's type to better summarize the underlying data, and change the display properties of text and numbers in a chart. What's more, you can add text boxes and legends to provide information that either doesn't appear in the underlying data or is difficult to summarize visually.

Creating a Chart

Access tables store lots of raw data—contact names, sales figures, prices, salaries, and so on. Raw numbers are great for calculations but aren't ideal when you need to describe the data to another human being. Charts and graphs, which summarize data visually, enable you to communicate data values and trends, whether for your own use or for inclusion in a business report.

Build a New Chart

1. Open a blank form in Design view.

2. If necessary, click the Design tab.

3. Click the Controls group's More button and then click the Chart button.

4. Drag the mouse pointer to define the chart's area.

5. Select the option button to display your database's tables, queries, or both.

6. Click the table or query to provide chart data.

7. Click Next.

8 Click the first field to add to the chart.

9 Click the Add button.

10 Repeat steps 8 and 9 to add more fields to the chart.

11 Click Next.

12 Click the desired chart type.

13 Click Next.

14 Verify that the chart appears the way you want it to and then click Next.

15 Type a name for the chart.

16 Select the option button that reflects whether you want to display a legend or not.

17 Click Finish.

Caution

When you view a form or report with a chart in Design view, the chart might not reflect the data you used to create it. Don't panic! When you switch to Form view for a form (Preview view for a report), the chart will be correct.

Tip

You can see what your chart will look like by clicking the Preview Chart button at the top left of the wizard page.

Formatting Chart Elements

Charts present your data visually, so take the time to format your chart elements so it presents your data collection in its best light. Access 2010 lets you change the appearance of any chart element, which means that you can change the chart's appearance to match your corporate color scheme, the data stands out, and the axes and explanatory text complement the data effectively.

Change an Element's Fill Color

① Open the form in Design view.

② Double-click the chart.

③ Click the chart element you want to format.

④ On the Formatting toolbar, click the Fill Color button's down arrow.

⑤ Click the desired color.

 Tip

If you don't see the Fill Color button on the Standard toolbar, hover your mouse pointer over the left edge of the Formatting toolbar, just to the left of the Font control. Drag the Formatting toolbar down until it occupies a second row in the toolbar area.

Change an Element's Font, Size, and Style

① Open the form in Design view.

② Double-click the chart.

③ Click the chart element you want to format.

④ Using the controls on the Formatting toolbar, follow any of these steps:

  • Click the Font control's down arrow and click the desired font.

  • Click the Font Size control's down arrow and click the desired size.

  • Click the Bold, Italic, or Underline button to apply or remove the style.

Change an Element's Number Format

① Open the form in Design view.

② Double-click the chart.

③ Click the chart element you want to format.

④ Using the controls on the Formatting toolbar, follow one of these steps:

- Click the Accounting Number Format button to apply the Accounting number format.

- Click the Percent Style button to display the number as a percentage.

- Click the Comma Style button to display the number using commas as a thousands separator.

- Click the Increase Decimal or Decrease Decimal button to add or remove decimal places from the number.

Customizing Chart Axes

Access charts summarize numerical data, such as sales figures, project labor costs, class attendance, grades, and donations received. Typically, you can divide your data into a set of categories, such as product types, projects, or months. The structure of the table or query that provides data for your chart determines how your chart appears, but you can decide whether to add a title to identify the types of values displayed on the horizontal or vertical axis. You can also make it easier to compare values on your chart by displaying or hiding the gridlines that mark values on the vertical axis and categories on the horizontal axis.

Add a Title to an Axis

1. Open the form in Design view.

2. Double-click the chart.

3. On the menu bar, click Chart.

4. Click Chart Options.

5. If necessary, click the Titles tab.

6. Follow either or both of these steps:

   - Type a title for the horizontal axis in the Category (X) Axis box.

   - Type a title for the vertical axis in the Value (Y) Axis box.

7. Click OK.

Tip

The smaller the chart you create, the more likely you will want to turn gridlines off.

Show or Hide Axis Gridlines

① Open the form in Design view.

② Double-click the chart.

③ Using the controls on the Standard toolbar, follow either of these steps:

- Click the Category Axis Gridlines button to show or hide the horizontal axis's gridlines.

- Click the Value Axis Gridlines button to show or hide the vertical axis's gridlines.

Add Information to a Chart

As much as you might like to think your Access 2010 chart data is self-explanatory, adding contextual information to your chart's form helps your audience understand the chart's data. A legend, which lists both the data series displayed in a chart and the colors used to represent the series, allows chart viewers to associate the chart's contents with your organization's results. You can also add text boxes that contain explanatory text to emphasize specific aspects of your data or to provide information not easily communicated in a chart.

Show or Hide a Chart Legend

1. Open the form in Design view.

2. Double-click the chart.

3. On the Standard toolbar, click the Legend button.

Change the Legend's Location

1 Open the form in Design view.

2 Double-click the chart.

3 On the menu bar, click Chart.

4 Click Chart Options.

5 If necessary, click the Legend tab.

6 Select the Placement option that represents where you want the legend to appear.

7 Click OK.

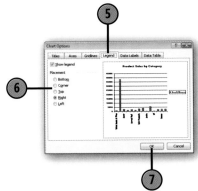

Add a Text Box

① Open the form in Design view.

② Double-click the chart.

③ On the Standard toolbar, click the Drawing button.

④ Click the Text Box button.

⑤ Drag the mouse pointer to define the text box.

⑥ Type the text to appear in the text box.

Changing a Chart's Type

Organizations store data of all kinds: stock reports, sales figures, department profits, information technology expenditures, and so on. Different data types demand different presentations, so you need to select the most appropriate chart type for your data. Access 2010 enables you to create 18 different types of charts, so you can experiment with your form to discover the chart type that summarizes your data most effectively.

Select a Different Chart Type

1. Open the form in Design view.

2. Double-click the chart.

3. On the Standard toolbar, click the Chart Type button's down arrow.

4. Click the desired chart type.

12

Interacting with Other Programs

Microsoft Access 2010 is a powerful program, but it doesn't try to do everything. Other programs in the Microsoft Office 2010 suite have complementary strengths: Microsoft Word 2010 is great for creating text documents, Microsoft Excel 2010 is ideal for recording and analyzing financial information, and Microsoft PowerPoint 2010 lets you convert your thoughts into attractive presentations you can print out or project onto a screen for audiences of hundreds or even thousands. You can also add images you create in a graphics program or capture with a scanner or digital camera.

Access 2010 also gives you a lot of versatility in interacting with other companies or individuals who might not keep their databases in Access 2010. You can easily export your Access 2010 table data and query results into lots of other file formats or bring in data from the same programs.

Introducing Linking and Embedding

Access 2010 works wonderfully as a stand-alone program, but it really shines when you use it in combination with other programs. One way to use Access 2010 in conjunction with other programs is to include files created in other programs, such as graphics, text documents created in Word 2010, PowerPoint 2010 presentations, or Excel 2010 charts and worksheets in your forms and reports. You can add these objects to your database through linking and embedding.

Linking and embedding are done through the same dialog box, but there are several important things you need to keep in mind when you decide whether to link to an object or to embed it in a form or report. As the name implies, embedding an object in a form or report stores a copy of the object with the database. For example, if you want to add a company logo to an invoice generated from table data, you could identify the graphic and indicate you want to embed it in the database. The advantage of embedding an object in a database is that you never have to worry about the graphic, chart, or spreadsheet not being available because the person pulling up the form or report has copied the database to a computer without the embedded file. If you create databases with embedded files, you can travel anywhere, secure in the knowledge that the files will be there.

The downside to embedding objects in databases is that the embedded files can be quite large and increase the size of the database file significantly. While a single, low-resolution logo meant to be viewed on a computer monitor probably won't have much of an impact on your file size, the same image rendered at a resolution suitable for printing might double the size of the database. If you embed more than one image or more than one copy of the same image, you might make your database unworkably large.

When you want to include more than one image or external file in an Access 2010 database, the best choice may be to create a link to the files in the form or report. For example, rather than embed many copies of a high-resolution logo in your reports, you could save the file on your computer and link to the file's location on your computer. Access 2010 uses the reference to find the file and display it as part of a database object. The database is no larger than it was originally, and you don't need to have multiple copies of the same document if you link to it more than once. So, the advantage of linking is that you save hard drive space, but the disadvantage is that moving from computer to computer can be difficult unless you take the non-Access 2010 files with you when you travel. In general, you should embed an object in an Access 2010 database if you use the object once and you have room to store the database (with the only included object) when you travel. In other cases, such as when you use the same file multiple times in the same database, consider linking to the file and not embedding it.

Inserting a New Object

Access 2010 tables and queries hold a lot of data, but you can augment your Access 2010 data with information in files created with other programs. For example, you might create a Word 2010 document with important background information or a PowerPoint 2010 presentation that puts your data into context for your colleagues. You can include those files in your Access 2010 forms and reports by linking or embedding the files as objects.

Embed an Existing Object

1. Open a form or report in Design view.

2. Click the Design tab.

3. Click the Controls group's More button and then click the Unbound Object Frame button.

4. Drag on the body of the form to define the frame's boundaries.

5. Select the Create from File option.

6. Click Browse.

7. Navigate to the folder that contains the target file.

8. Click the target file.

9. Click OK to close the Browse dialog box.

10. Click OK to close the Microsoft Access dialog box.

Link to an Existing Object

1. Open a form or report in Design view.

2. Click the Design tab.

3. Click the Controls group's More button and then click the Unbound Object Frame button.

4. Drag on the body of the form to define the frame's boundaries.

5. Select the Create from File option.

6. Click Browse.

7. Navigate to the folder that contains the target file.

8. Click the target file.

9. Click OK to close the Browse dialog box.

10. Select the Link check box.

11. Click OK to close the Microsoft Access dialog box.

Tip

If you want to link or embed an object but don't want it to take up much space on the form or report, select the Display as Icon check box to display the file's Windows icon instead of the object itself.

Manipulating Objects

Once you add an object to a form or report, you can work with it in the same way you work with form or report controls. For example, if you want to display the same image at the top and bottom of a report, you could do so by adding the image to the report, copying it, and then pasting it at the bottom of the report. If the object you created isn't in the right position or isn't the correct size, you can move or resize it so that it fits into your form or report in exactly the right way.

Copy an Object

1. Display a form or report in Design view.

2. Click the object you want to copy.

3. Click the Home tab.

4. Click the Copy button.

Paste an Object

① Display a form or report in Design view.

② Click the Home tab.

③ Click the Paste button.

Move an Object

① Display a form or report in Design view.

② Drag an object to its new location.

Resize an Object

① Display a form or report in Design view.

② Click the object you want to resize.

③ Position the mouse pointer over an edge or corner of the object.

④ Drag the edge or corner until the object is the desired size.

See Also

For more information about rearranging your objects on a form or report, see "Setting Control Appearance" on page 152.

Inserting Excel 2010 Charts and Worksheets

Access 2010 is designed to let you store, manipulate, and ask questions of large amounts of data. Excel 2010 offers a wide range of data analysis and presentation tools you can use to extend the analysis you perform in Access 2010. Including an Excel 2010 chart or worksheet in an Access 2010 form or report lets you explore alternative scenarios, use past data to project future patterns, or summarize your data in ways not available in Access 2010 summary queries.

Add an Excel 2010 Chart

① Open a form or report in Design view.

② Click the Design tab.

③ Click the Controls group's More button and then click the Unbound Object Frame button.

④ Drag on the body of the form to define the frame's boundaries.

⑤ If necessary, select the Create New option.

⑥ Click the Microsoft Excel Chart object type.

⑦ Click OK.

Tip

The Excel Chart control is an Excel 2010 workbook that contains a worksheet and a chart sheet. To change the data displayed in the chart, click the Sheet1 worksheet tab and edit the data there.

Add an Excel 2010 Worksheet

1. Open a form or report in Design view.

2. Click the Design tab.

3. Click the Controls group's More button and then click the Unbound Object Frame button.

4. Drag on the body of the form to define the frame's boundaries.

5. If necessary, select the Create New option.

6. Click the Microsoft Excel Worksheet object type.

7. Click OK.

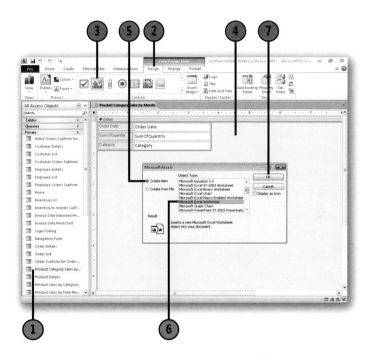

Importing Data from Another Access 2010 Database

One way to think of an Access 2010 database is as a collection of facts about a particular subject. For example, you could have a database that tracks your sales contacts and correspondence, another database that tracks your product inventory, and yet another that tracks your vehicles and the miles they drive. It makes sense to separate your data into topic-based databases, but there are times when a table from one database is useful in another database. For example, if you want to use data from a table in a database that's hosted on another computer, consider importing that data into your own database to guard against the network being down or the database being unavailable. Access 2010 also lets you save the import operation so you can repeat the steps quickly the next time you want to import the same table or tables.

Import One or More Tables

1. Click the External Data tab.

2. In the Import & Link group, click Access.

3. Select the Import Tables, Queries, Forms, Reports, Macros, And Modules Into The Current Database option.

4. Click Browse.

5. Navigate to the folder that contains the database from which you want to import a table.

6. Double-click the database.

7. Click OK.

8. Click the Tables tab.

9. Click the tables you want to import.

10. Click OK.

11. Select the Save Import Steps check box.

12. Type a name for the import operation.

13. If desired, type a description for the import operation.

14. Click Save Import.

Caution

Importing a table from another database means you don't have to type the data a second time, but you must be sure either that the copied table's contents won't change or that it doesn't matter if the table's contents do change. If the table's contents change regularly, the absolute worst thing you can do is create a second version of the same table. For example, if you start tracking sales contacts in two databases, everyone needs to know that the separate tables exist and where to find them. Not only would they have to enter the data twice but there would also be twice as many opportunities for data entry errors.

See Also

For information on linking to a table in another database, see "Linking to a Table in Another Access 2010 Database" on page 196.

Linking to a Table in Another Access 2010 Database

When you first start using Access 2010, it can be tempting to store all your data about everything in a single database. The names and addresses of sales contacts could live beside the list of product categories, but they really shouldn't. It's better to create separate databases to store data on specific subjects, such as products or sales leads. If you do need to use data from one database in another database, you can do so. For example, if you track active customers in your orders database, you can use the same table in your sales contacts database. Access 2010

enables you to create links to tables in other databases. Linking to another table means that every change made to the table in the original database, or in the database with the link, appears in the table. Unlike when you copy a table from one database to another, linking ensures that the data is available to everyone who needs it.

Create a Link to a Table

1. Click the External Data tab.

2. In the Import & Link group, click Access.

3. Select the Link To The Data Source By Creating A Linked Table option.

4. Click Browse.

5. Navigate to the folder that contains the target database.

6. Double-click the target database.

7. Click OK.

8. Click the tables to which you want to create a link.

9. Click OK.

> **Tip**
>
> Access 2010 displays the linked table with all your database's other tables, but the linked table's icon has a right-pointing arrow at its top-left corner, indicating that it's a linked table.

Working with Hyperlinks

A fundamental characteristic of the World Wide Web is the ability to create connections—called *hyperlinks*—between related documents. By creating hyperlinks to helpful files on the Web, or even to objects in the current Access 2010 database, you can provide useful information to anyone viewing the page. Those documents may in turn have links that lead you away from the main document. You can easily return to the database page quickly by clicking your Web browser's Back button or, if a hyperlink leads to a Web page viewed in a Web browser, you can simply switch back to the Access window. Hyperlinks to Web pages start with http://, but a hyperlink to a file in the same directory as the database consists of just the file's name. If the file name occurs in a field with the Hyperlink data type, Access 2010 knows to display the file name as a hyperlink.

Create a Hyperlink to an Existing File

1. Display a form or report in Design view.

2. Click the Design tab.

3. Click the Hyperlink button.

4. Click Existing File Or Web Page.

5. Navigate to the folder that contains the file to which you want to link.

6. Click the file to which you want to link.

7. Type a short phrase to describe the hyperlink's target.

8. Click OK.

Create a Hyperlink to a Web Page

1. Display a form or report in Design view.

2. Click the Design tab.

3. Click the Hyperlink button.

4. Click Browsed Pages.

5. Click the page to which you want to link.

6. Type a short phrase to describe the hyperlink's target.

7. Click OK.

If you know the URL of the Web page to which you want to link, you can type it directly into the Address box of the Insert Hyperlink dialog box.

Create a Hyperlink to an Existing Database Object

① Display a form or report in Design view.

② Click the Design tab.

③ Click the Hyperlink button.

④ Click Object In This Database.

⑤ Click the show detail control next to the desired object type.

⑥ Click the database object to which you want to link.

⑦ Type a short phrase to describe the hyperlink's target.

⑧ Click OK.

Importing Data from an Excel 2010 File

On the surface, Excel 2010 and Access 2010 look a lot alike. Both programs handle data lists effectively. In fact, some small-business owners maintain all their data lists in Excel 2010 and use that program's summary functions, sorting, and filtering capabilities as if Excel 2010 were a database program. That's fine if you have a single data table you want to analyze, but there's no easy way to create relationships between tables, define queries using filters, or generate reports. Fortunately, there's a straightforward process you can follow to bring an Excel 2010 data list into Access 2010. Once your Excel 2010 data is in a database, you can create reports and queries that are possible, but very hard, to create in Excel 2010.

Import Excel 2010 Data

1. Click the External Data tab.

2. In the Import & Link group, click Excel.

3. Select the Import The Source Data Into A New Table In The Current Database option.

4. Click Browse.

5. Navigate to the folder that contains the desired Excel 2010 file.

6. Double-click the file.

7. Click OK.

8. Click the type of data sources you want to display.

9. Click the specific source from which you want to draw your data.

10. Click Next.

11. If the first row of the Excel 2010 table contains the desired column headings, select the First Row Contains Column Headings check box.

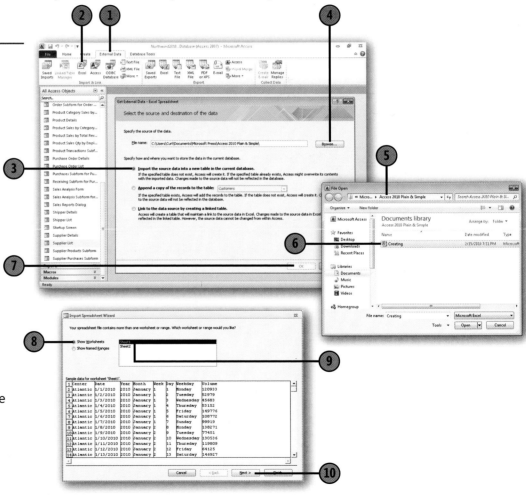

12 Verify that the data appears to be arranged correctly and click Next.

13 Click the data column you want to edit.

14 If desired, type a new name for the field.

15 Click the Indexed box's down arrow, and select whether you want the field to be indexed and whether to allow duplicate values.

16 Click the Data Type box's down arrow, and select the field's data type.

17 If necessary, repeat steps 13 through 16 for other fields you want to edit.

18 Click Next.

19 Select the option that indicates how you want Access 2010 to assign a primary key to the table.

20 If necessary, select the Choose My Own Primary Key option box's down arrow and click the field to use as a primary key.

21 Click Next.

22 Type a name for the new table.

23 Click Finish.

Caution

If the Excel 2010 workbook from which you want to copy data contains a single worksheet and no tables or named data ranges, you won't see the wizard page that asks you to identify the data source.

Tip

If you don't want to import a field, display the Field Options page of the Import Spreadsheet Wizard, click the target field, and select the Do Not Import Field (Skip) check box.

Importing Data from a Text File

In the early days of personal computing, it was very hard to transfer data between programs and, in some cases, between computers. Different computers used different types of disks, programs created files that no other programs could read, and organizations developed solutions that didn't enable information workers to collaborate effectively. However, most programs knew how to deal with data stored as a text file. That's still the case today. If you absolutely must work with data from a program that can't create another data format Access 2010 understands, you can always have your colleagues export their data as a text file. Access 2010 knows how to convert text files to database tables, which then enables you to integrate the new data into your database.

Import Text Data

1. Click the External Data tab.

2. In the Import & Link group, click Text File.

3. Select the Import The Source Data Into A New Table In The Current Database option.

4. Click Browse.

5. Navigate to the folder that contains the desired text file.

6. Double-click the file.

7. Click OK.

8. Select the option button that reflects whether the source file's data contains field delimiters or whether the fields contain fixed numbers of characters.

9. Click Next.

10 Select the option that reflects the delimiter character.

11 If necessary, select the First Row Contains Field Names check box.

12 Click Next.

13 Click the data column you want to edit.

14 Type a new name for the field.

15 Click the Indexed box's down arrow and select whether you want the field to be indexed and whether to allow duplicate values.

16 Click the Data Type box's down arrow and select the field's data type.

17 If necessary, repeat steps 13 through 16 for other fields you want to edit.

18 Click Next.

19 Select the option button that indicates how you want Access 2010 to assign a primary key to the table.

20 Click Next.

21 Type a name for the new table.

22 Click Finish.

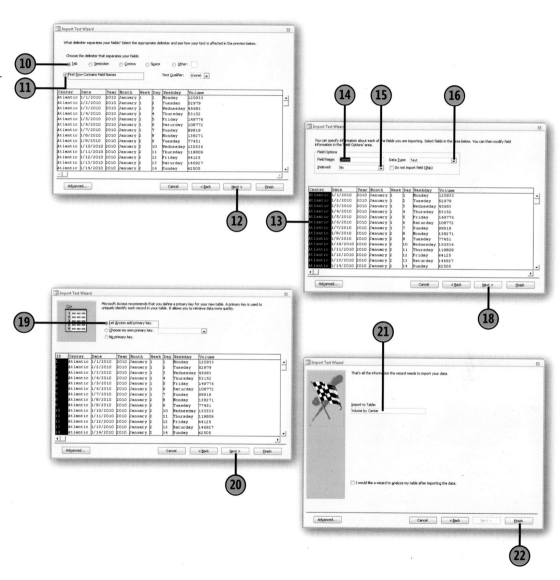

Importing Data from an XML File

It's easy to find data analysis programs such as Access 2010 and Excel 2010 that know how to read data from text files into their native formats. Text files have a couple of important limitations, though. The first limitation is that the files don't contain any formatting details, so any conditional formats, cell colors, or text formatting is lost when you import the data into Access 2010. Similarly, text files don't contain any information describing the data in the file. Sure, you can create a text file that has information about the file's data (who created it, and so on), but Access 2010 imports the data into the table and forces you to delete the nonsense rows, or you have to strip the data from the file before importing the data.

Some really bright folks combined the flexibility of text files with a scheme to include information about a file's contents within the file. The Extensible Markup Language (XML) enables you to save a database table as a text file that contains elements, called tags, which describe the file's contents. What's great about the XML format is that if Access 2010 finds a tag it doesn't understand, it ignores it and keeps on importing the file's data.

Import XML Data

1. Click the External Data tab.

2. In the Import & Link group, click XML File.

3. Click Browse.

> **Tip**
>
> If a table with the same name as the XML file already exists in the database, Access 2010 adds a number to the end of the name. For example, if you import an Orders table and your database contains a table with that name, Access 2010 names the new table Orders1. Importing the XML file again results in a table named Orders2, and so on.

④ Navigate to the folder that contains the desired XML file.

⑤ Double-click the file.

⑥ Click OK.

⑦ Click the table that contains the data you want to import.

⑧ Click OK.

⑨ Select the Save Import Steps option.

⑩ Type a name for the saved import operation.

⑪ If desired, type a description for the saved import operation.

⑫ Click Save Import.

Tip

If you import an XML file with the same name as an existing database table, you can select the Append Data to Existing Table(s) option in the Import XML dialog box to have Access 2010 add the data to the existing table.

Exporting Data to a Text File

At the most basic level, database tables are collections of text. Company names? Text. Order identifiers? Text. Sales amounts? Text. Yes, you can attach nontextual files such as images to Access 2010 database records, but the directions to those files' locations on your computer or network can always be expressed using text. Most programs know how to process files stored as text, so if you need to interact with a colleague or vendor who is using an older database system or custom application that doesn't interact well (or at all) with Access 2010, export your table or query to a text file and let him or her work with your data in the most universal form available.

Export Text Data

① Click the table you want to export.

② Click the External Data tab.

③ In the Export group, click Text File.

④ Click Browse.

Tip

Database data can occasionally contain commas, so I recommend that you use the Tab character to delimit data you export to text files.

(5) Navigate to the folder where you want to save the text file.

(6) Type a name for the file.

(7) Click Save.

(8) Click OK.

(9) Select the Delimited option.

(10) Click Next.

(11) Select the option that represents the delimiter character you want to separate the fields.

(12) Select the Include Field Names on First Row check box.

(13) Click Finish.

(14) Select the Save Export Steps option.

(15) Type a name for the saved export operation.

(16) If desired, type a description for the saved export operation.

(17) Click Save Export.

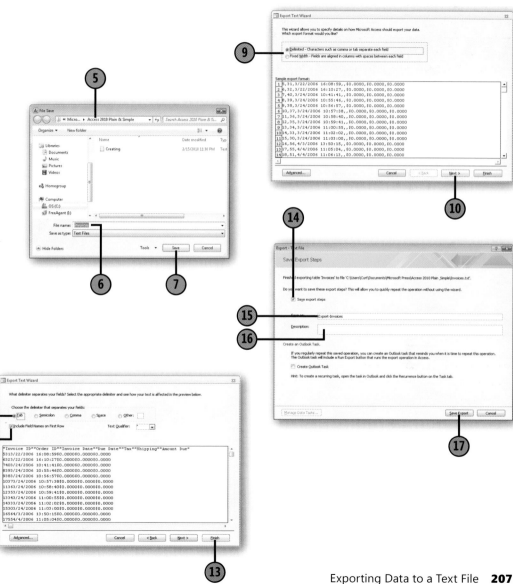

Exporting Data to Another Access 2010 File

Dropping all your paper-based reports, articles, and research into a single file folder doesn't make much sense. Gathering absolutely all your information into one place is better than throwing it away, but it's only a marginal improvement. Instead, it makes more sense to group your organization's data into distinct databases that each focus on a particular subject. If you are a school administrator, you can use Access 2010 to track your students' attendance. Businesses can manage employees' time cards, sales contacts, and the company's product inventory in Access 2010, but it makes sense to create a separate database for each function. If you need to use data from one Access 2010 database in another database, you can transfer your data table without any trouble.

Export to Another Access 2010 Database

1 Click the object you want to export to another database.

2 Click the External Data tab.

3 In the Export group, click Access.

4 Click Browse.

⑤ Navigate to the folder with the target database.

⑥ Click the name of the database.

⑦ Click Save.

⑧ Click OK.

⑨ Type a name for the object.

⑩ Click OK.

⑪ Select the Save Export Steps option.

⑫ Type a name for the saved export.

⑬ If desired, type a description for the export.

⑭ Click Save Export.

Tip

If you type the name of an object that already exists in the target database, Access 2010 offers you the choice of replacing the existing object or typing a new name for the object you're exporting.

Exporting Data to an XML File

Most programs are able to make use of data stored in text files, but plain text files don't let you store formatting information, data validation rules, or whether a field allows users to only append data to existing values. However, XML provides the means to encode that information into the body of a text file using tags. These tags indicate where a table row begins, where each cell begins and ends, each column's data type, any data validation rules applied to the column, and so on. The files Access 2010 creates contain a lot of information that is specific to Access 2010, but because Access 2010 creates files with tags most other programs can process, the information about your file usually translates between programs just fine.

Export XML Data

1 Click the object you want to export to another database.

2 Click the External Data tab.

3 In the Export group, click XML File.

4 Click Browse.

5. Navigate to the folder where you want to save the data file.

6. Type the file name.

7. Click Save.

8. Click OK.

9. Verify that the Data (XML) and Schema Of The Data (XSD) check boxes are selected.

10. Click OK.

11. Select the Save Export Steps option.

12. Type a name for the saved export.

13. If desired, type a description for the export.

14. Click Save Export.

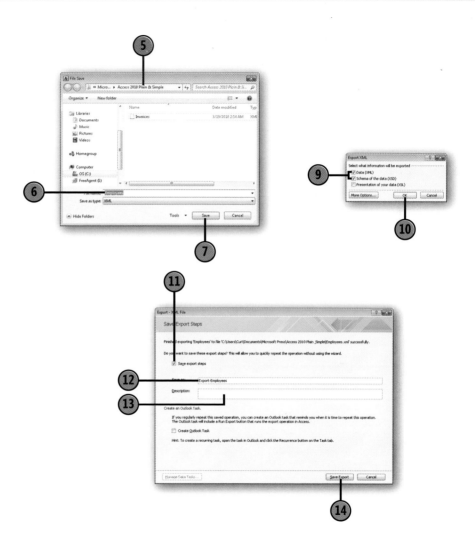

Saving Database Objects As Web Files

One of the easiest ways to communicate data to traveling colleagues is to make that data available on a Web page. Writing the data to a Web page means you don't have to send the entire database file to the traveler. In fact, your colleague doesn't even need Access 2010 on his or her machine! Saving database objects as Web pages is also a great way to make data available over a corporate network (an intranet). So long as your company's network supports Web connections, you can make your data available to any authorized user.

Save an Object As a Web File

① Click the object you want to save as a Web file.

② Click the External Data tab.

③ In the Export group, click More.

④ Click HTML Document.

Tip

The HTML Output Options dialog box appears when you save a Form or Report. Those objects have Office Themes applied to them; the HTML Output Options dialog box contains tools you can use to select the output options, including changing the Web file's theme.

(5) Click Browse.

(6) Navigate to the folder where you want to store the Web file.

(7) If desired, type a new name for the file.

(8) Click Save.

(9) Click OK to close the Export-HTML Document dialog box.

(10) If it appears, click OK to close the HTML Output Options dialog box.

(11) Select the Save Export Steps check box.

(12) Type a name for the saved export.

(13) If desired, type a description for the saved export.

(14) Click Save Export.

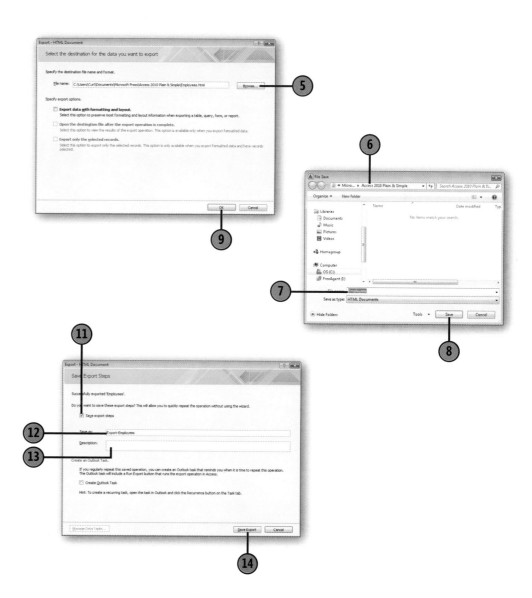

Analyzing Data with Excel 2010

Each of the programs in the Office 2010 suite has its particular strengths, but Excel 2010 and Access 2010 have a lot of similarities. Both programs handle data lists well, but where Excel 2010 shines at summarizing data using an incredible variety of calculations and formulas, Access 2010 enables you to create powerful queries to draw exactly the data you need from your tables.

If you have a table or query that contains exactly the data you want to analyze and summarize in Excel 2010, using summary functions and operations not readily available in Access 2010, step through the following procedure to bring the power of Excel 2010 to bear on your data.

Analyze Data in Excel 2010

1. Click the table or query you want to analyze.

2. Click the External Data tab.

3. In the Export group, click the Excel button.

4. Click Browse.

5 Navigate to the folder where you want to create the Excel 2010 workbook.

6 Type a name for the file.

7 Click Save.

8 If desired, select the Export Data With Formatting And Layout option.

9 Click OK.

10 Select the Save Export Steps option.

11 Type a name for the saved export.

12 If desired, type a description for the export.

13 Click Save Export.

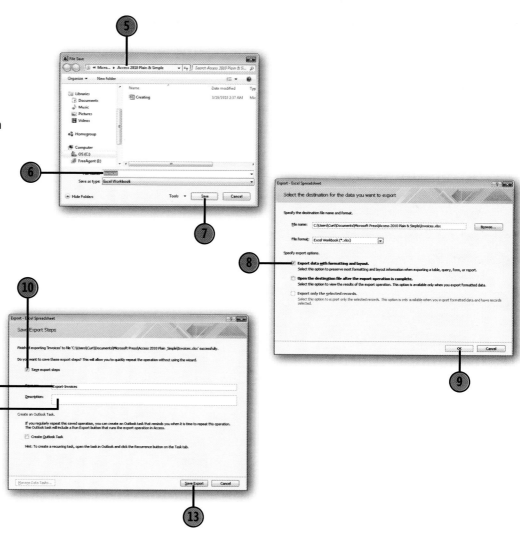

Publishing Data to Word 2010

You've probably used Word 2010 to create documents in your office or at home. Word 2010 is great for general correspondence, creating mass mailings, and designing attractive newsletters, but it's not the program you want to use to store large data lists. Yes, you can store data in Word 2010 tables, but it's hard to do more than the most rudimentary summaries of that data. Access 2010 makes it much easier for you to summarize and find subsets of your data. Then, whether your data is destined to be included in an annual report, a briefing to your boss, or a letter documenting all open invoices with a specific vendor, Access 2010 enables you to transfer your data to a Word 2010 document efficiently.

Export Data to Word 2010

1 Click the table or query you want to export.

2 Click the External Data tab.

3 In the Export group, click the More button.

4 Click Word.

5. Click Browse.

6. Navigate to the folder where you want to create the Word 2010 document.

7. Type a name for the file.

8. Click Save.

9. If desired, select the Open The Destination File After The Export Operation Is Complete option.

10. Click OK.

11. Select the Save Export Steps option.

12. Type a name for the saved export.

13. If desired, type a description for the export.

14. Click Save Export.

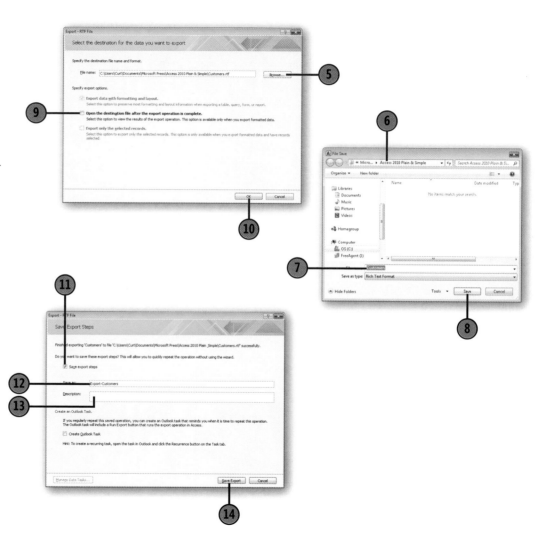

Collecting Data from E-mail Messages

Gathering data from one's colleagues, vendors, and customers can be a frustrating process. When you ask a question by phone, in person, or over e-mail, you end up transcribing the responses and typing them into your database. The potential for inaccuracies, mistranscriptions, and other mistakes abound. One useful task you can perform in Access 2010 is to create Microsoft Outlook 2010 messages that contain Access 2010 forms. You send the form to a colleague as an e-mail message, which the recipient fills out and sends back. You can then read the data directly from Outlook 2010 into your Access 2010 table. You never have to touch the data with your hands, which means that you don't have to worry about making a mistake as you type the data. Yes, it's possible your colleague made a mistake while entering their responses, but you reduce the number of steps in the process and eliminate many opportunities to introduce errors.

Send a Data Collection E-Mail Message

1. Click the table for which you want to collect data.

2. Click the External Data tab.

3. In the Collect Data group, click Create E-Mail.

4. Click Next to advance past the first Collect Data Through E-Mail Messages wizard page (not shown).

5. Select the HTML Form option.

6. Click Next.

7. Select the Collect New Information Only option.

8. Click Next.

9. Click the first field you want to add to the form.

10 Click the Add button.

11 Repeat steps 9 and 10 to add all applicable fields.

12 Click Next.

13 Verify that the Automatically Process Replies And Add Data To Customers option is deselected.

14 Click Next.

15 Select the Enter The E-mail Addresses In Microsoft Outlook option.

16 Click Next.

17 Type a subject for the e-mail messages.

18 Type an introduction for the e-mail messages.

19 Click Next.

20 Click Create.

Caution

If you select the Automatically Process Replies And Add Data To *Table* option, Outlook 2010 exports any survey replies to your Access 2010 table when the messages arrive. However, if the database is open when Outlook 2010 attempts to write the data to your table, the operation will fail, and you will need to transfer the data manually.

Process Data Collection E-Mail Messages

1 Close the Microsoft Access database into which you want to bring in the form data.

2 In Microsoft Outlook 2010, click the Inbox mailbox name.

3 Click the message folder that contains the form replies.

4 Right-click the data collection message.

5 Click Export Data to Microsoft Access.

6 Click OK twice to export the data and to dismiss the message box that appears to indicate the data transfer was successful.

13

Administering a Database

When working with sensitive data, you need to ensure that only authorized individuals are able to read it. For example, if you manage a database containing your co-workers' salary information and performance reviews, you should do as much as you can to keep the database in good working order and ensure that no one has access to that information unless it is needed.

Microsoft Access 2010 has a range of security and administration tools you can use to protect sensitive data while still allowing folks with a legitimate need to get at the data with as little hassle as possible. Those tools range from requiring your colleagues to type passwords to use a database to the Documenter utility that prints the vital statistics of every object in your database.

Introducing Database Security

At their heart, databases are programs to store important data. Whether you're protecting your friends' privacy by ensuring that no one else opens your contacts database or preventing your colleagues from accidentally modifying or deleting important business data, database security is a critical part of using Access 2010 on computers connected to a network.

Passwords

Because they're so important to good security, in Access 2010 and elsewhere, a quick note about passwords is in order. The best passwords are random strings of characters, but random characters are hard to remember. One good method of creating hard-to-guess passwords is to combine elements of two words, mixing uppercase and lowercase letters with a number in between to generate a character string that is at least eight characters long. For example, if you know something about horseback riding, you might have a password of StiRr03rt, which could be read as "stirrups, three notches higher on the right." In any event, avoid passwords that are simple dictionary words in English or any other language, as they can easily be solved by password-guessing programs available on the Internet. Substituting numbers for letters in dictionary words, as in c00l, is no better as all substitutions are included in the password-guessing programs.

Encrypting Databases

Another technique you can use to prevent unauthorized users from getting at your data is to encrypt the database. When you create a database, the data and structural information used to create the database is stored as plain text, which can be read quickly and easily. The problem is that the same information can be read by opening the file in a word processor. So, even if you set user accounts and passwords for your database, it's still possible to read the underlying data. To prevent unauthorized viewing, you can scramble the information used to create the database. Access 2010 can read the data without difficulty, but the database runs about 10 to 15 percent slower because of the additional processing required.

Encrypting a Database

When you create an Access 2010 database, you should consider that it's possible to view and edit the contents of an Access 2010 database using a word processing program such as Microsoft Word. You don't see the tables in the same easy-to-use layout you get when you open the database in Access 2010, but all the data is there. In other words, storing your database on a computer without Access 2010 is no guarantee your data is safe from prying eyes. Fortunately, obscuring the contents of your database, or encrypting the database, can be accomplished in just a few steps.

Encrypt a Database

① Close any open databases.

② Click the File tab.

③ Click Open.

④ Click the database you want to open.

⑤ Click the down arrow at the right edge of the Open button.

⑥ Click Open Exclusive.

⑦ Click the File tab.

⑧ Click Encrypt with Password.

⑨ In the Set Database Password dialog box that appears, type your password.

⑩ Retype your password.

⑪ Click OK twice to assign the password and acknowledge the message box that appears.

Caution

If you don't open your database in Exclusive mode, clicking the Encrypt with Password button causes Access 2010 to display a warning dialog box instructing you to close the database and reopen it in Exclusive mode.

Decrypt a Database

① Click the File tab.

② Click Decrypt Database.

③ In the Unset Database Password dialog box, type the database's password.

④ Click OK.

> **Caution**
>
> Decrypting a database also turns off password protection.

Locking Database Records

Forms are versatile objects—you can use them to browse a database table or your query results, or to enter or modify table records. There may be some forms, however, that let your colleagues peek into tables where the records are too important to be modified. To prevent accidents where important data gets deleted by well-meaning computer users, you can set a form's properties so the ability to add, modify, and delete records is turned off.

If more than one person is responsible for entering data into your database, you could run into a situation where more than one person attempts to enter or edit data using a form. Attempting to edit records simultaneously can result in data entry errors, so it's best to prevent a user from editing a record when another user is trying to do the same thing.

Prevent More than One User from Editing a Form Record

1 Open a form in Design view.

2 Double-click the form selector.

3 Click Data.

4 Click Record Locks.

5 Click the down arrow that appears.

6 Click Edited Record.

Tip

Clicking the Record Locks down arrow and then clicking All Records prevents users, including yourself, from making any changes to the form's data.

Lock Records in a Form

① Open a form in Design view.

② Double-click the form selector.

③ Click Data.

④ Follow these steps for the Allow Additions, Allow Deletions, and Allow Edits properties:

- Click the property name.

- Click the down arrow that appears.

- Click No.

Creating a Navigation Form

When you open some databases, a navigation form appears to help you find commonly used database forms and reports. You can also create a custom navigation form by hand. Access 2010 comes with a number of navigation form templates you can use to build the most effective tool for your users. After you create a blank navigation form, you can add tabs and then populate them with database objects.

Create a Navigation Form

① Click the Create tab.

② Click Navigation.

③ Click the type of navigation form you want to create.

④ Click the Save button.

⑤ Type a name for your navigation form.

⑥ Click OK.

Add an Object to a Navigation Form

① Open a navigation form in Layout view.

② Drag an object from the Navigation Pane to the Add New tab.

Change the Appearance of a Navigation Form Tab

① Open a navigation form in Layout view.

② Click the tab you want to format.

③ Click the Format tab.

④ Use the controls on the Format tab to change the appearance of the form tab.

Move a Navigation Form Tab

① Open a navigation form in Layout view.

② Move your mouse pointer over the tab you want to move so the mouse pointer changes to a four-way arrow.

③ While the mouse pointer appears as a four-way arrow, drag the item to the desired position.

Caution

Don't forget to save your navigation form! When you create another type of form but haven't saved it yet, Access 2010 gives it a name such as Form1. However, when you create a navigation form, the name Navigation Form appears on the form's tab in the Access 2010 program window, so it can appear that the form has already been saved.

Tip

You can delete a navigation form tab by displaying the form in Layout view, right-clicking the tab, and then clicking Delete.

Tip

You can identify the type of data a navigation form object contains by changing its tab color or shape. For example, customer information tabs could be blue rectangles, sales data could be red circles, and so on.

Documenting a Database

Keeping track of every table, query, and report in a database isn't that hard when the database is new and fresh in your memory, but as you add new objects and move on to other projects, it can be hard to remember everything about your database. Access 2010 can document the properties of selected objects in your database by running the Documenter. In the

Documenter, you can choose the objects you want to get information about and then print a report, which gives you both a hard copy of your database in case something goes wrong and a report you can pass on to a programmer or administrator should you move on to other projects.

Document a Database

1. Click the Database Tools tab.

2. Click Database Documenter.

3. Click the dialog box tab representing the objects you want to document.

4. Follow any of these steps to select the objects you want to document:

   - Select the check box next to an object to select the object (you can also click an object's name and then click the Select button).

   - Click Select All to select every listed object.

   - Click Deselect All to remove all your previous selections.

5. Click OK.

Caution

If you document every element of your database, the printed report could be extremely long.

Try This!

Open the Northwind sample database and click the Database Tools tab. In the Analyze group, click Database Documenter to display the Documenter dialog box. In the Documenter dialog box, click the Tables tab, click the Employees table, click Select, and then click OK. Access 2010 creates a report detailing the selected objects.

Setting Startup Options

When you create a database for you and your colleagues to enter data, you may want to limit what your colleagues can do with the database. Locking records and assigning database passwords provide some restrictions, but you can also set which form appears when you start the database and limit users to use the built-in menus. When you create a database where users see only a designated form at startup, you've created an application.

Change an Application Title

1. Click the File tab.

2. Click Options.

3. Click Current Database.

4. Type a title for the Application.

5. Click OK.

Caution

Clicking (None) on the Display Form/Page drop-down menu means that no form opens when you or your colleagues run the database. If you hide the database window on startup, your colleagues won't be able to view the database's contents!

Hide All Menus

① Click the File tab.

② Click Options.

③ Click Current Database.

④ In the Ribbon and Toolbar Options section, deselect the Allow Full Menus check box.

⑤ Deselect the Allow Default Shortcut Menus check box.

⑥ Click OK.

Set Startup Form

1. Click the File tab.

2. Click Options.

3. Click Current Database.

4. In the Application Options section, click the Display Form down arrow.

5. Click the form you want to appear when the database opens.

6. Click OK.

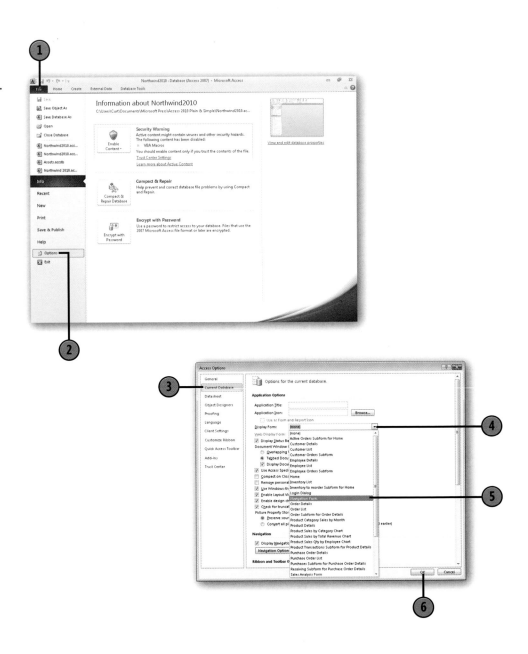

Set Startup Display Options

1 Click the File tab.

2 Click Options.

3 Click Current Database.

4 Deselect the Display Status Bar check box to hide the status bar.

5 Deselect the Display Document Tabs check box to hide the tabs of open documents.

6 Deselect the Enable Layout View for this Database check box to prevent users from displaying forms and reports in Layout view.

7 In the Navigation section, deselect the Display Navigation Pane check box to prevent users from displaying the database's objects.

8 Click OK.

14

Customizing Access 2010

In this section:

- **Adding Commands to the Quick Access Toolbar**
- **Modifying the Ribbon User Interface**

Microsoft Access 2010 is designed so you can create and use your databases quickly and easily. As you get more familiar with the program, you may find that you perform some tasks more frequently than others, or that you'd work more effectively if the Quick Access Toolbar or the Ribbon were set up a little differently. You can modify how Access 2010 presents itself to you to make your work flow quickly.

One way you can change the Access 2010 interface is to add or remove buttons from the Quick Access Toolbar. Clicking the Customize Quick Access Toolbar button, located at the right edge of the Quick Access Toolbar, shows a list of all buttons available for that toolbar. If there are buttons on the Quick Access Toolbar that you don't use as much as you used to, it's no trouble to remove them. Access 2010 also provides the new capability to create custom Ribbon tabs, add individual commands or groups of commands to the Ribbon, change the order of the Ribbon tabs, and hide tabs without deleting them.

Finally, Access 2010 attempts to detect when you make a spelling error and offers to replace the misspelled word with what it believes is the correct word. You can control which terms are replaced by following a few straightforward steps.

Adding Commands to the Quick Access Toolbar

The vast majority of commands you'll use in Access 2010 appear on the Ribbon, but some of the commands require you to move through one or two levels of the user interface (for example, click the correct Ribbon tab and then click a button to open a dialog box). If there's a specific command you use all the time, you can make that command easier to find by adding it to the Quick Access Toolbar. If you later find that you don't use the command as much as you used to, you can always remove the command and make room for the commands you do use.

Add a Command to the Quick Access Toolbar

1. Right-click any command on the Quick Access Toolbar.

2. Click Customize Quick Access Toolbar.

3. Click the Choose Commands From down arrow.

4. Click the category from which you want to choose the command.

5. Click the command you want to add.

6. Click Add.

7. Click OK.

Tip

To display the Quick Access Toolbar page of the Access dialog box while you are in Backstage view, on the File menu, click Options and then click Quick Access Toolbar.

Remove a Command from the Quick Access Toolbar

(1) Right-click any command on the Quick Access Toolbar.

(2) Click Remove from Quick Access Toolbar.

Move the Quick Access Toolbar

(1) Right-click any command on the Quick Access Toolbar.

(2) Click the Show Quick Access Toolbar below the Ribbon command.

Tip

You can change the order of the buttons on the Quick Access Toolbar by displaying the Quick Access Toolbar page of the Access Options dialog box, clicking the command you want to move, and then clicking either the Move Up or Move Down button.

Tip

You can also add a button on the Ribbon to the Quick Access Toolbar by right-clicking the button and choosing Add To Quick Access Toolbar.

Modifying the Ribbon User Interface

Access 2010 enhances your ability to customize the entire Ribbon user interface. The Ribbon consists of several elements: tabs, which are designated by the clickable words at the top of the Ribbon (e.g., Home, Create, External Data, and Database Tools); groups, which are named collections of commands (such as the Text Formatting group on the Home tab); and commands, which are individual items within a group (such as the Bold button in the Home tab's Text Formatting group).

In Access 2010, you can hide and display Ribbon tabs; reorder tabs, groups, and commands displayed on the Ribbon; customize existing tabs (including Tool tabs, which appear when specific items are selected); and create custom tabs.

Add a Command to a Ribbon Tab

① Right-click any Ribbon tab.

② Click Customize the Ribbon.

③ Click the tab to which you want to add the command.

④ Click the Choose Commands From down arrow.

⑤ Click the category from which you want to choose the command.

⑥ Click the command you want to add.

⑦ Click Add.

⑧ Click OK.

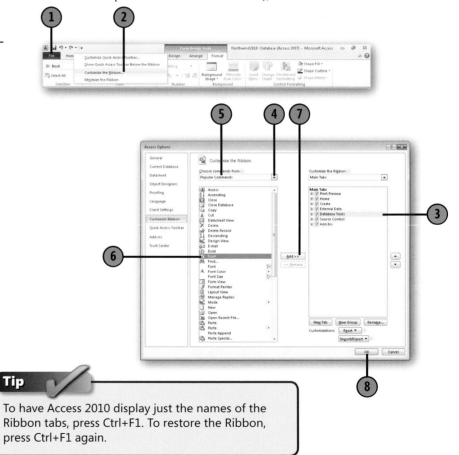

Tip

To restore the Ribbon to the same configuration it had when you installed Access 2010, right-click anywhere on the Ribbon, click Customize the Ribbon, click Reset, click Reset All Customizations, and then click OK. If you just want to remove the changes from a specific Ribbon tab, click that tab in the right pane, click Reset, click Reset Only Selected Ribbon Tab, and then click OK.

Tip

To have Access 2010 display just the names of the Ribbon tabs, press Ctrl+F1. To restore the Ribbon, press Ctrl+F1 again.

Reorder Commands on a Ribbon Tab

① Right-click any Ribbon tab.

② Click Customize the Ribbon.

③ Click the command, group, or tab you want to move.

④ Click the Move Up or Move Down button.

⑤ Click OK.

Tip

If a command is in the last position on a tab and you click the Move Down button, Access 2010 places the command in the first position of the next tab.

Remove a Ribbon Element

① Right-click any Ribbon tab.

② Click Customize the Ribbon.

③ Click the command, group, or tab you want to remove.

④ Click Remove.

⑤ Click OK.

Caution

Removing a custom tab or group deletes that element. If you want the element to remain available for use, hide it instead of removing it.

Create a Custom Ribbon Tab

1 Right-click any Ribbon tab.

2 Click Customize the Ribbon.

3 Click the tab above where you want the new tab to appear.

4 Click New tab.

5 Click OK.

Try This!

Right-click anywhere on the Ribbon and then click Customize the Ribbon. In the right pane, click the Insert tab and then click New Tab. Then, from the command list in the left pane, click Font, and then click Add. When you click OK to close the Access Options dialog box, a tab named New Tab appears on the Ribbon. When you click the New Tab tab, you'll see that it contains a group named New Group, which in turn contains the Font command.

Add a New Group to a Ribbon Tab

1 Right-click any Ribbon tab.

2 Click Customize the Ribbon.

3 Click the group or tab name above where you want the new group to appear.

4 Click New Group.

5 Click OK.

Tip

Don't feel the need to fill up your custom Ribbon tab. If you use five groups of commands and they fit in the left half of the tab, you should leave the rest of the custom tab empty.

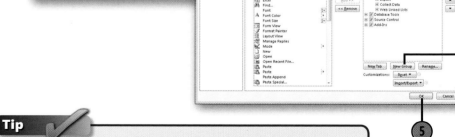

Rename a Ribbon Element

① Right-click any Ribbon tab.

② Click Customize the Ribbon.

③ Click the element you want to rename.

④ Click Rename.

⑤ Type a new name for the element.

⑥ Click OK.

⑦ Click OK.

Tip

When you rename a custom Ribbon command, the Rename dialog box displays a set of icons. Selecting one of the icons helps you identify the element visually.

Hide a Ribbon Element

① Right-click any Ribbon tab.

② Click Customize the Ribbon.

③ Clear the check box next to the item you want to hide.

④ Click OK.

Redisplay a Hidden Ribbon Element

1. Right-click any Ribbon tab.

2. Click Customize the Ribbon.

3. Select the check box next to the item you want to display.

4. Click OK.

Changing AutoCorrect Options

You're bound to make typing mistakes when you spend a lot of time at the keyboard. In fact, slowing down doesn't help; the slower you go, the more likely you are to hit the wrong keys as you try to guide your fingers to the keys using your eyes instead of letting your muscle memory take over. Over the years, many users have allowed the programming team to monitor their typing, which means that the Access 2010 team

has been able to identify the most common mistakes resulting from popular misspellings, letter transpositions, and errors that are the result of not hitting the Spacebar fast enough to put a space between words. If one of the words Access 2010 identifies as an error is actually correct (for example, you work with a client corporation named Idae, a popular misspelling of the word idea), you can delete that entry from the AutoCorrect list.

Change AutoCorrect Options

① Click the File tab.

② Click Options.

③ Click Proofing.

④ Click AutoCorrect Options.

⑤ Deselect the check boxes next to the rules you want to turn off or select the check boxes next to the rules you want to turn on.

⑥ Click OK to close the AutoCorrect dialog box.

⑦ Click OK to close the Access Options dialog box.

Tip

To undo an Auto-Correct correction, press Ctrl+Z.

Tip

Many users type the same text frequently, such as "Payment is due within 30 days. If payment is made within 10 days, you may deduct 2% from the total amount due." If you often type that text, you could create an AutoCorrect entry that replaces the phrase Net30_2 with the text describing the payment terms listed.

Add AutoCorrect Rules

(1) Click the File tab.

(2) Click Access Options.

(3) Click Proofing.

(4) Click AutoCorrect Options.

(5) Type the text to be replaced.

(6) Type the text to replace the previous entry.

(7) Click Add.

(8) Click OK to close the AutoCorrect dialog box.

(9) Click OK to close the Access Options dialog box.

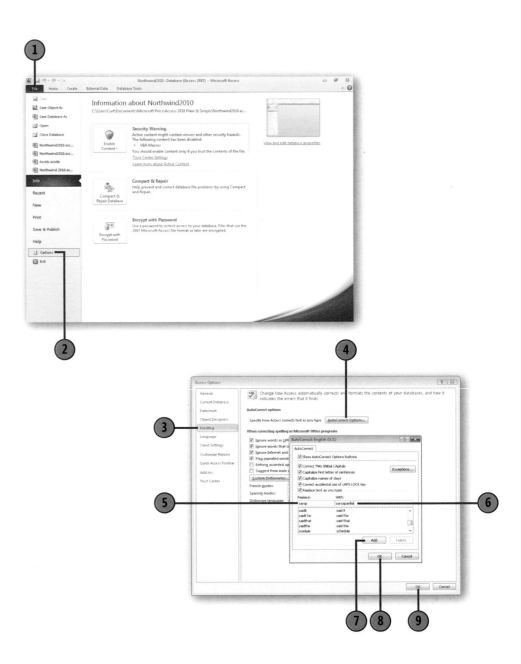

Delete an AutoCorrect Entry

1 Click the File tab.

2 Click Options.

3 Click Proofing.

4 Click AutoCorrect Options.

5 Click the entry to be removed.

6 Click Delete.

7 Click OK to close the AutoCorrect dialog box.

8 Click OK to close the Access Options dialog box.

15

Presenting Table and Query Data Dynamically

Microsoft Access 2010 places wide-ranging and powerful capabilities at your disposal. You can build tables to store data effectively, ask questions of the data using queries, and display the data in forms and reports. Even better, you can use many of those techniques in a single database object: the Pivot-Table Report.

When you create a PivotTable, you build a versatile object you can use as part of live business presentations to illustrate your own points and answer your colleagues' questions quickly. If you'd rather summarize your data visually, you can create Pivot-Chart Reports, which let you reorganize and redisplay your data in a chart.

Introducing PivotTables and PivotCharts

Access 2010 gives you a lot of flexibility in choosing how to present your data. The most basic method of presenting your data is in a table, where the data is listed one row at a time. Displaying your data in a form lets you present the data one record at a time; reports give you the additional ability to organize your table contents or query results based on grouping levels. Finally, if one field in your table or query is related to two other fields in the table or query, such as with sales data for the quantity of a given product sold in a month, you can create a crosstab query to present the data in relation to the other fields.

PivotTables let you combine all these abilities into a single database object, with some added benefits thrown in. Not only can you present your data in an easily understood format but you can also change the data's organization while you have the PivotTable open. As with other database objects, Access 2010 steps you through the PivotTable creation process with a wizard that explains everything you need to do.

Pivoting

When you open a form that contains a PivotTable, your data appears in a layout that is very similar to that of a Crosstab query. PivotTables add to this by enabling you to reorganize the data in the PivotTable by moving the field heads to reflect the desired layout.

Field heads

Filtering

When you work with large data collections, it's important that you be able to limit the data that appears on the screen. With PivotTables, you can click the down arrow at the right edge of a field head and choose the values to display.

Once you choose the values you want to concentrate on, clicking OK limits the contents of the PivotTable to the items you selected.

PivotCharts

Just as you can create PivotTables, which let you reorganize your table data, you can create PivotCharts to summarize your data graphically. As with a PivotTable, you can change how the PivotChart presents your data, both by reorganizing the data and by changing the PivotChart's chart type.

Creating a PivotTable

Access 2010 databases let you gather and present important data, but the standard table shows only a list of values. Forms and reports enable you to summarize and display your data so it's easier to evaluate, but you're still limited to a single view of your data. Even queries, which let you perform calculations on your data or present it in a crosstab worksheet, provide just a single view of your data. PivotTables, by contrast, let you rearrange your data dynamically. If your PivotTable lists sales by category, and you'd rather see the data organized by country, you can change the layout of your PivotTable quickly. Once you create your first PivotTable, you understand how powerful a tool it is!

Create a PivotTable Form

① Click the table or query that contains the data you want to summarize in your PivotTable.

② Click the Create tab.

③ Click More Forms.

④ Click PivotTable. If necessary, click the body of the PivotTable form to display the Field List.

Tip

You should add every field from the table or query you're using to your PivotTable. You won't need to use all of the fields in the PivotTable, but they will be available if you do want them.

⑤ If necessary, click the body of the PivotTable form to display the Field List. Drag fields that you want to provide values for the PivotTable's rows from the PivotTable Field List box to the Drop Row Fields Here area.

⑥ Drag fields that you want to provide values for the PivotTable's columns from the PivotTable Field List box to the Drop Column Fields Here area.

⑦ Drag the fields that you want to provide values for the body of the PivotTable from the PivotTable Field List box to the Drop Totals or Detail Fields Here area.

⑧ Click the Save button.

⑨ Type a name for the PivotTable form.

⑩ Click OK.

Tip

When you create a PivotTable, you should rename it to ensure that "PivotTable" appears in the name of the form you create to hold it. Changing a form's name doesn't change how it functions, but it does make it easier to find.

See Also

For information about using the Drop Filter Fields Here area, see "Filtering PivotTable Data" on page 255.

Adding and Removing PivotTable Fields

After you create a PivotTable, you can arrange the fields on the PivotTable to present your data effectively. It is possible your colleagues could ask questions you hadn't thought of, but that you could answer if you included another field in the PivotTable and used it to filter or organize your data. Maybe they're interested in how dairy products have been selling in South America. While you didn't include the countries for each

sale in the original PivotTable design, that data is in the query on which you based the PivotTable. All you need to do is add it to the design. By the same token, you can remove any fields you're not using. You can drag them from the body of the PivotTable to the PivotTable Field List box, ready for use if you need them again.

Add a Field to a PivotTable

1. Display the forms in your database.

2. Double-click the PivotTable form.

3. If necessary, click the Field List button.

4. Drag the field you want to the desired spot on the PivotTable.

Tip

If the Field List box doesn't appear when you click the Field List button, click anywhere in the body of the PivotTable form to display it.

Remove a Field from a PivotTable

① Display the forms in your database.

② Double-click the PivotTable form.

③ Right-click the field header of the field you want to remove.

④ Click Remove.

Pivoting a PivotTable

Perhaps the biggest benefit of presenting your data using PivotTables is that you can change the data's organization on the fly, creating literally dozens of different forms from a single data set! All you have to do is drag the header of the field you want to move to its new position. When you release the mouse button, Access 2010 examines the PivotTable's new structure and rearranges the data to match it. If previously you had listed sales by Country and then by product Category, you could drag the Category field header to the left of the Country field header to reverse the grouping.

Reorganize PivotTable Data

1. Display the forms in your database.

2. Double-click the PivotTable form.

3. Drag the header you want to relocate to the desired position in the PivotTable.

Tip

If you use a lot of fields in your PivotTable, you might not be able to remember the exact ordering of fields that produce a particular arrangement. When you find an arrangement that presents your data effectively, send yourself an e-mail message with the order or record the arrangement in a Word document so you can re-create the arrangement quickly.

Filtering PivotTable Data

When you create a PivotTable from the data in your tables or queries, you often have several screens worth of data to move through. Reorganizing your data can help you interpret your data, but you can also filter your PivotTable by choosing the data you want to see. For example, if your PivotTable shows sales data for a series of products grouped by category, you can pick the categories for which you want to view data.

Select Which Field Values to Display

1. Display the forms in your database.

2. Double-click the PivotTable form.

3. Click the down arrow on the header of the field by which you want to filter.

4. Deselect the All check box to clear the check boxes for all values.

5. Select the check box next to any value you want to display.

6. Click OK.

Tip

If you're not sure whether all values in a field are displayed, look at the field's header. The down arrow will be blue if the field has a filter applied to it.

Filter by a Field Not Displayed in the Body of a PivotTable

1. Display the forms in your database.

2. Double-click the PivotTable form.

3. If necessary, click the Field List button.

4. Drag the field by which you want to filter the PivotTable to the Drop Filter Fields Here area.

5. Click the down arrow on the field header.

6. Deselect the All check box.

7. Select the check box next to each value to display.

8. Click OK.

Toggle a Filter On and Off

1. Click the AutoFilter button to remove a filter.

2. Click the AutoFilter button again to reapply the filter.

Formatting a PivotTable

PivotTables are all about presenting your data effectively, and a significant element of any presentation is the appearance of your data. To change the appearance of an element of your

PivotTable, such as the color, pattern, and font, you use the Properties box.

Change a PivotTable's Appearance

1. Display the forms in your database.

2. Double-click the PivotTable form.

3. Click the part of the PivotTable you want to format.

4. Click the Property Sheet button.

5. Set the format you want in the Properties box.

6. Click the Close box.

Tip

You can format another PivotTable element without closing the Properties box. Click OK to apply the formatting to the current element and then click the next element you want to change. The Properties box changes to reflect the new element.

Caution

Any changes you make in Design view won't appear in Pivot-Table view.

Creating a PivotChart

Just as you can create tables that you can reorganize on the fly to emphasize different aspects of your table and query data, you can also create dynamic charts, or PivotCharts, to summarize your data effectively. By changing the grouping order of the fields used to create your PivotChart, or by limiting which values are presented in the PivotChart, you answer specific questions posed by you and your colleagues. In addition to letting you change how your data appears in the chart, you can even change the type of chart you use to display your data!

Step through the PivotChart Wizard

1. Click the database object that contains the data you want to summarize using a PivotChart.

2. Click the Create tab.

3. Click More Forms.

4. Click PivotChart.

⑤ Drag fields that you want to provide values for the PivotChart's category axis rows from the Chart Field List box to the Drop Category Fields Here area.

⑥ Drag fields that you want to provide values for the PivotChart's data series from the Chart Field list box to the Drop Series Fields Here area.

⑦ Drag the fields that you want to provide values for the body of the Pivot-Chart from the Chart Field list box to the Drop Filter Fields Here area.

⑧ Click the Save button.

⑨ Type a name for your PivotChart.

⑩ Click OK.

Change a PivotChart Chart Type

1. Display the forms in your database.

2. Double-click the form that contains your PivotChart.

3. If necessary, click the Design tab.

4. Click the Change Chart Type button.

5. Click the Type tab.

6. Click the new chart type.

7. Click the subtype of the chart you want to create.

8. Click the Close box.

Index

date picker controls
    adding to forms, 98
    hiding, 98
Date/Time data type, 51
Decrease Decimal button, 178
Decrease Horizontal option, 153
Decrease Vertical option, 154
decrypting databases, 224
default values
    setting, 59
defining
    relationships, 44–45
deleting. *See also* removing
    AutoCorrect entries, 245
    controls from forms, 95–97
    fields, 48
    group levels (reports), 140
    navigation forms, 228
    Office Clipboard items, 76
    primary key, 48
    report controls, 135–136
    tables
        from Relationships window, 44
    text, 75
    themes, 149
descriptions
    fields, 33–34, 34, 35
design
    databases
        field descriptions, 33–34, 34
        foreign keys, 27
        primary key, 27
        tables with single objects, 26
    tables
        many-to-many relationships, 43
design grid
    removing tables from, 112

Design view, 48
    adding pictures to reports/forms,
        162–163
    charts, 175
    creating forms in, 90, 91
    creating queries, 112
    creating reports, 132
    creating tables in, 33–34
    editing queries, 110–112
    lines, 157
    modifying forms, 93
    Office themes, 147
Detail section (reports), 138
dialog boxes
    Import Objects
        importing data from database
            objects, 41
displaying. *See also* hiding
    axis gridlines, 180
    chart legends, 181
    datasheets with forms, 101
    Field List, 94
    Field List task pane, 133
    fields
        tables, 94
    forms with datasheets, 101
    gridlines, 158–159
    query results, 105, 126
    Quick Access Toolbar, 236
    Ribbon elements, 242
display options
    setting, 233
Division operator, 114
Documenter
    documenting databases, 229
documenting databases, 229
documents (Word 2010)
    exporting data to, 216–217

drawing
    lines
        forms/reports, 156
duplicate queries
    finding, 117, 118

E

editing
    field properties, 52–53
    forms, 93, 94
    input masks, 57
    queries
        in Design view, 110–112
    reports, 133–134
    text, 75–76
e-mail messages
    sending data collections, 218–220
embedding, 186–191
    existing objects, 187–188
    pictures, 162–163
encrypting databases, 222–224
enforcing
    referential integrity, 45
Equal Horizontal option, 153
Equals operator, 114
Equal Vertical option, 154
Etched special effect, 153
Excel 2010, 185
    charts
        inserting into databases, 192–193
    data analysis, 214–215
    importing data into databases, 200
    worksheets
        inserting into databases, 192–193

R

W

Web Browser control, 97
Web databases, 7
Web files
   saving objects as, 212–213
Web pages
   creating hyperlinks to, 198
   hyperlinks, 197–199
Web sites
   Office.com, 31
     finding templates online, 32
Whole Field option, 70, 71
width
   columns, 79
   images, 170–171
wizards
   adding controls to forms, 95
   Create Relationship, 38
   Form Wizard
     creating forms, 89

Import Spreadsheet, 201
Input Mask, 57
Label
   creating mailing labels, 142–143
   line breaks, 143
PivotChart
   creating PivotCharts, 258–260
Query Wizard
   creating queries, 106–109
Report
   creating reports, 128–129
Subform Wizard, 99
Word 2010, 185
   publishing data to, 216–217
workbooks (Excel 2010)
   importing data into databases, 200–201
worksheets (Excel 2010)
   importing data into databases, 200–201
   inserting into databases, 192–193

X

XML files
   exporting data to, 210–211
   importing data into databases, 204–205
XOR operator, 114

Y

Yes/No data type, 51

Z

zero-length strings
   disallowing, 58

About the Author

Curtis D. Frye is the author of *Microsoft Office Excel 2007 Step by Step*, *Microsoft Excel Version 2007 Plain & Simple*, several books on Microsoft Access, and numerous online training courses. He is a coauthor of *Microsoft Office Excel 2003 Programming Inside Out*.

What do you think of this book?

We want to hear from you!

To participate in a brief online survey, please visit:

microsoft.com/learning/booksurvey

Tell us how well this book meets your needs—what works effectively, and what we can do better. Your feedback will help us continually improve our books and learning resources for you.

Thank you in advance for your input!

Stay in touch!

To subscribe to the *Microsoft Press® Book Connection Newsletter*—for news on upcoming books, events, and special offers—please visit:

microsoft.com/learning/books/newsletter